Sailors
AND Sailing Adventures

Poems, Commentaries, and Short Stories

CLEON MCCLAIN

iUniverse, Inc.
Bloomington

Sailors and Sailing Adventures
Poems, Commentaries, and Short Stories

Copyright © 2013 by Cleon McClain.

All rights reserved. No part of this book may be used or reproduced by any means, graphic, electronic, or mechanical, including photocopying, recording, taping or by any information storage retrieval system without the written permission of the publisher except in the case of brief quotations embodied in critical articles and reviews.

iUniverse books may be ordered through booksellers or by contacting:

iUniverse
1663 Liberty Drive
Bloomington, IN 47403
www.iuniverse.com
1-800-Authors (1-800-288-4677)

Because of the dynamic nature of the Internet, any web addresses or links contained in this book may have changed since publication and may no longer be valid. The views expressed in this work are solely those of the author and do not necessarily reflect the views of the publisher, and the publisher hereby disclaims any responsibility for them.

Any people depicted in stock imagery provided by Thinkstock are models, and such images are being used for illustrative purposes only.
Certain stock imagery © Thinkstock.

Library of Congress Control Number: 2013908962

ISBN: 978-1-4759-9141-3 (sc)
ISBN: 978-1-4759-9142-0 (ebk)

Printed in the United States of America

iUniverse rev. date: 06/03/2013

CONTENTS

Acknowledgement ix
Introduction xi

Ch. 1   Commentary on "The Conversation" 1
Ch. 2   Commentary on "The Dream?" 8
Ch. 3   Commentary on "Old Man in a Rocking Chair" 15
Ch. 4   Commentary on "Welcome Aboard!" 22
Ch. 5   Commentary on "The Lady Mae" 29
Ch. 6   Commentary on "The Mouse!" 35
Ch. 7   Commentary on "Autumn Evening" 41
Ch. 8   Commentary on "A Boat Without a Name" 47
Ch. 9   Commentary on "The Treasure" 58
Ch. 10 Commentary on "A Sailor's Wife" 63
Ch. 11 Commentary on "This is Good—All is Well" 70
Ch. 12 Commentary on "The Visit" 75
Ch. 13 Commentary on "Me, My Brother, and Friend" 83
Ch. 14 Commentary on "Eleven Tears of the Lord" 90

Appendices 97
  Introduction 97
  The Glenda Kay 99
  Sailing Greenleaf Lake 102
  Lake Tenkiller Adventure 107

About the Author 115

For

Glenda

My wife, my love, my friend.
Without her help, encouragement, support, and inspiration,
this book would never have been possible.

ACKNOWLEDGEMENT

I would like to thank my wife Glenda. Without your love and encouragement, this book would never have been written. You are the source of my inspiration, my friend, and the love of my life. My love, appreciation, and thankfulness I have for you is beyond my ability to express in words. Thank you Sweetie.

I would like to thank my parents and brother. Although we are now separated by death or circumstances, I will always cherish the memories that we share together. Among those memories are all the times we spent at the lake. It was during those times that I developed my love for the water, water sports, and sailing. I love and thank each one of you.

I will forever be grateful to Ron Williams, a close friend from my college days, who I have consulted with, and received advice from numerous times in the process of writing this book. Your knowledge, encouragement, and unselfish help was invaluable. This book would never have been possible without it. Thank you Ron.

My acknowledgements would not be complete without thanking my life-long friend Jerry MacLean. You have supported me in all my endeavors throughout my life. We played football together, you were at my wedding, with me at the death of my father, and all the times in between and beyond. I love you like a brother, and I thank you.

Cleon McClain

Last, but certainly not least, I would like to thank you who bought my book. A book is not worth the pages it is printed on if it is not read. The fact that you have chosen to give your time to read my book is the greatest compliment that anyone could give me. I thank you from the bottom of my heart.

INTRODUCTION

First and foremost, I would like to thank you for reading my collection of poems. It is my hope that as you read you will find at least one poem that speaks to you in such a way that you will want to read it again and again, and perhaps share it with a friend.

I have written these poems primarily for sailors or those interested in sailing. I hope however, that the selections of poems within this book might be enjoyed by many others who simply have an interest in, and a love for poetry. My style is simple and unsophisticated. If you are an acute student of poetry who counts syllables and study rhyme and meter, my poetry will probably be a disappointment to you. If however, you read poetry simply for enjoyment and relaxation, then my poetry may speak to you in a special way and give you hours of pleasure. For it is this reason I write poetry. I like to say my poetry is nothing more than a story that rhymes . . . hopefully! It is my wish that my straight-forward and easy to read style is refreshing, and appeals to your taste.

It has been my experience that many times it is helpful to understand what was going on in the life and mind of the poet at the time he was writing a poem, to better gain an appreciation of the poetry. With this thought in mind, each poem in the selections of this book will be preceded by a short commentary by me. The commentary will give a short explanation, information, or simply set the mood for the poem. I have also added some short stories about my current sailboat the *Glenda Kay* and some adventures we shared together, which are found in the appendices of this book. It is my hope that the commentaries, as well as the stories in the appendices will add to your reading pleasure.

I should mention at this time that I am a Christian and some of the poems reflect my faith. I think however, that these poems will be appreciated and definitely not be found to be offensive by those persons of other faiths. It is my deep belief that we are all on our own faith journey and all are deserving of respect and reverence. Consequently, I will never intentionally write anything that would be disrespectful of any religion.

As the title of this book indicates, all the poems (with the exception of one special poem) are about sailors or sailing adventures. Some of the poems were conceived from my own sailing exploits, while many were simply conjured up from my imagination. Whether the poem is grounded in fact or fiction, it is my hope that within these pages you will be carried away from the cares of this world to a land far away. Some of the poems may make you sad. Some may make you laugh. Others may leave you scratching your head wondering what that was all about. Whatever your reaction, my hope is that you enjoy what you are about to read and consider the following pages my gift to you.

Now find a soft comfortable chair. Throw another log on the fire. Get yourself a hot cup of tea. Open the pages of this book and prepare to let your imagination carry you away.

CH. 1

Commentary on "The Conversation"

The adventure of the sailboat in the poem "The Conversation" is purely fictional. The circumstances that initially gave me the idea behind the poem are grounded in my personal experience. My boat the *Glenda Kay* is only thirteen feet in length and twice we have been caught out sailing in wind gusting to 30 miles per hour! Thank goodness it was not raining at that time as it is in the poem. But, you can take it from me that sailing a thirteen foot boat in 30 miles per hour wind is a very scary way to spend the day! I think any small boat sailor that has been caught out sailing in such extreme conditions will be able relate to the fear the sailor in the poem is experiencing. I know I can.

When I wrote "The Conversation" I was thinking about the first time I sailed in high wind with the *Glenda Kay*. I remember how my mind raced. Knowing if I made a single mistake, it could be disastrous. Minutes seemed like hours. Unlike the sailor in the poem who continued to sail, I dropped all sails and motored the *Glenda Kay* into a cove, out of the wind, and anchored for the night. Thankfully, the wind blew itself out by the next morning.

Looking back on this experience, I have come to the conclusion that the *Glenda Kay* has often taken better care of me than I have of her. Like the man in the poem, I also find myself actually talking to myself and my boat while sailing in extreme weather. Just as the sailor in the poem patted the *Glenda Kay* and thanked her for bringing him home safely, so did I, on that day when the *Glenda Kay* and I found protection in that small cove.

When I started writing this poem I thought it would end at this point, with the sailor finding safety in a cove or marina. The poem however, just didn't seem to be complete. Something was missing. I felt like I had something far more important to say than just telling about a storm that the *Glenda Kay* survived, but what?

I find as I create a poem the original story line often comes from personal experience. Then often as the poem progresses, I see the poem is really about more than just something that happened to me. I can't really put it into words. It's a feeling I get when I read my poems that lets me know when the poem captures what is in my soul. It's like a song writer composing a song. The composer may know if he is going to compose a waltz, a love song, or an anthem. The composer may even, in his head, have an idea of how the song should sound. However, it's not until he actually writes the song and hears it played, that he knows if the song is complete and expresses the feelings he wants in the song. Like the song writer who hears his music played can feel in his being it is not complete and needs more work. I knew and could feel in my being that my poem needed more work. I decided the poem should continue and not end with the boat in the safety of a cove or marina, as I originally planned. Ultimately, I saw the poem was not about the battle between the sailor and the storm at all. No, it was about much more than that. The real story eventually developed into a conversation the sailor has with a wealthy man at the dock.

It was at this point I started thinking about the time I joined a yacht club. Being a retired teacher, I was not in the same economic class as most of the members of the club. The members themselves were a great bunch of sailors, and many of them knew far more about sailing than I knew. As you might guess, the *Glenda Kay* being only thirteen feet long was by far the smallest boat in the fleet. It was also the butt of many of their jokes such as: "Did that boat come with a wind-up key, or let's put that boat in the clubhouse and fill the cockpit with ice for our beer"? I heard them all. I know the jokes were all in fun, and the fact that they even allowed me to join the club shows they were not snobs. I stayed in the club for only one year. They were a good bunch of sailors, but it just wasn't for me. I tend to be a loner and not much for parties and social events. While I was a member of the club however, I did meet a snob or two. I also found they tended to be the people that usually caused trouble. They wanted to run the show, and when things did not go their way, they griped and complained the most. When it came time for workdays at the club these people were never around, but you could always count on them being there for all the social events. This is what gave me the idea of the sailor in the poem, to have a conversation with one of these snobs.

At this point in the poem the small boat sailor meets a wealthy man. The wealthy man immediately makes fun of the sailor's small boat. Why would this wealthy man insult a perfect stranger like this? Did he think it would impress the small boat sailor because his sailboat was larger? Maybe the wealthy man just needed to reinforce his own self-worth at the expense of the small boat sailor. It might be something else. You decide as you read the poem. Then, when the small boat sailor turns down the wealthy man's invitation for dinner, the wealthy man gets mad. Why? I think it was because the wealthy man just could not understand how someone like this little boat sailor could have the nerve to say no to an important man like him. I also think he was eaten up with jealousy at the same time. For the wealthy man could see that this small boat sailor had something that he could never buy with all of his money. The wealthy man saw that the small boat sailor was very contented with his small boat and did not even desire a large yacht. He loved his small boat, loved sailing, and loved life. The wealthy man only had a passion for power, money, and possessions. In fact, the small boat sailor actually felt sorry for the wealthy man with his big sailboat and all the money in the world. The last line in the poem says it all, when the small boat sailor thinks of himself as being rich and the wealthy man as being poor. For me, this is a classic story of money can't buy happiness. Contentment has to come from being thankful for what you have, and not from keeping up with the Jones's. The thing is, as much as I would like to relate to the small boat sailor, I have to admit that I see myself in both men. I think if we are honest we all do. I am ashamed to admit it, but I still at times, find myself thinking I'm just a little better than the other guy. I sometime find myself taking pride in something I own, because it is a little better than what someone else has. So as I read this poem I think about myself. Who am I today? Am I the wealthy snob or am I the man I would like to be? How about you?

Please, for your reading pleasure, enjoy—"The Conversation."

A small boat sailor survives a horrible storm. He then sails into a marina and has a conversation with a wealthy sailor.

THE CONVERSATION

The wind was howling making an awful sound.
My boat was like a horse bucking up and down.
The rain, like bullets, was pelting my face.
A million thoughts in my head, how my mind raced!

The boat I sailed was tiny but stout.
Would we survive? How would it turn out?
The name of my boat is the *Glenda Kay*.
Only thirteen feet long, but proud and brave.

We were in a fight, this time for our life.
The *Glenda Kay's* bow sliced the water like a knife.
The waves were like mountains with tops frothy white.
Although mid-day, it was dark as night.

A flash of light! The crack of thunder!
I ducked my head and began to wonder.
When will this end? It has got to stop!
The clouds above swirled like a top.

Off in the distance I could see the sun shining.
Much different where I was—the wind still whining!
Spray covered my boat. My sails were soaked.
Yet the light in the distance gave me some hope.

Fighting the storm, we sailed towards the sun.
In the lee of mountains, the fight finally won.
The sky became blue. The wind abated.
Now sailing calm waters, I was elated.

I looked back and could see the storm raging on,
But over my bow, the sea was calm.
I patted the *Glenda Kay* and laughed out loud.
You're quite-a-boat old girl. You make me proud.

We sailed into a harbor, then into a marina,
Where large boats at buoys pirouette like ballerinas.
The large boats I saw all had looks of despair.
They were floating hotels, never sailing anywhere.

I sailed the *Glenda Kay* to the dingy dock,
And tied her with my favorite nautical knot.
I said to the *Glenda Kay,* "That was quite-a-sail!
Again you brought me home, alive and well."

A man came by with his wife and boy.
Dressed in designer clothes he yelled, "Ahoy!"
Not much of a boat you have, said he.
I own that fifty-footer, he said with glee.

I'm taking some steaks to my boat to grill.
You're welcome to come if only you will.
However be careful getting out of your boat.
It may tip over, he said as a joke.

As he got into his dingy, he saw the storm I survived.
It was moving away, but the man replied,
Looks like a bad one, I'd hate to be out there.
No boat could survive that—want your steak medium rare?

Thanks mister, but in my boat I'll eat beans from a can.
Enjoy your steak, I hope you understand.
Fine with me, the man snapped back.
People with small boats are strange—that's a fact!

To his wife he whispered, Can you believe that tiny boat?
It's a mystery to me that it can even float.
The small boat sailor thought, watching the wealthy man leave,
I wish that poor man was as rich as me.

        Cleon McClain

Cleon sailing the *Glenda Kay*—2005

CH. 2

Commentary on "The Dream?"

I remember one spring morning when I was a young boy in elementary school. I found myself in the basement of an old torn down house that was in a field behind where I lived. I was looking for a piece of wood, not just any piece of wood, but a piece of petrified wood. Earlier that week we studied in school about how petrified wood was made. When I woke up that morning, I just remembered I had put a piece of petrified wood in the basement of that old house. So, there I was rummaging through a damp smelly basement. I never found that piece of petrified wood, and I left the old house very disappointed. Someone must have stolen my petrified wood!

I've come to realize that I never put a piece of petrified wood in the basement of that old house. No, I simply had a dream. But, the dream was so real that when I woke up—I just knew I had put that petrified wood in that basement!

Dreams can be wonderful and take different forms. I just shared a dream I had long ago while I was sleeping, but we can also have dreams while we are awake. These are the dreams we usually have about things we would like to do, or accomplish. They can also be the dreams we have for our loved ones, our nation, and yes—even the world. These dreams are often the best kind of dreams and they are extremely important for us all to have. These are the dreams that give us hope and a reason to live. I honestly believe that when a person stops dreaming, that person starts to die. For if there is no dream, there is no hope, and without hope, what is the use of continuing?

I am 60 years old and I still have dreams. They are not the same dreams I had as a young man, for the time for most of those dreams have come and gone. There is a season for everything, and the dreams I now have are the dreams of an old man, but they keep me going. I even have one special dream that I have only shared with my wife. Will it come true? Who knows? Maybe—maybe not. The important thing is to have a dream that you can cling to, strive to achieve, or look forward to. Even as I write this commentary, I have a dream to publish a book of poems. Will it happen? I hope. I'm working on it now, and if you are reading this, then you are helping one of my dreams come true.

Dreams are powerful. Acting on a dream to make it come true is even more powerful, because that requires faith, the faith to think you can achieve your dream. Martin Luther King Jr. had that kind of faith. Gandhi had that kind of faith. Mother Theresa had that kind of faith. Need I go on? They all had the faith to pursue their dreams. We may not have a dream as grand as these people, but who knows where dreams can lead us? The collective small dreams of many of us working together may someday find the cure for cancer, stop hunger in our world, overcome hate, prejudice and bigotry, or who knows what else. Yes, dreams are powerful.

The dreams of children are very special because many of their dreams are centered on imagination. They may dream of being a pirate sailing the Caribbean searching for treasure, or flying a space ship to Mars in search for alien beings. I wonder how our lives would change if we adults could dream big like a child does? I don't mean that as adults we should still be dreaming about becoming a pirate, but how many of our dreams die just because we are told that we can't possibly achieve our dreams. How many of us have simply given up on a dream because we were not supported by a friend, parent, or loved one? We humans strongly want, and need, to have someone to believe in us and our dreams. But, we adults have been conditioned to buy into the notion that we must dream with our heads and not with our hearts. After all, imagination is fine for children, but not for us adults. I don't know, sometimes I question this rationale. I think our biggest dreams must incorporate imagination, and this is what we lose as we get older. We call it being grown-up. We adults, after all, have to be practical when we dream—or do we?

"The Dream?" is about an old sailor late at night sitting in a dark room in front of a fireplace. Outside large snowflakes are slowly drifting from the sky. The inside of the room is bathed by the soft light and warmth of the fireplace. I can imagine the old sailor just sitting and staring at the fire as it flickers, his mind a thousand miles away. He might be thinking of a day long ago when he was sailing into a beautiful lagoon with palm trees and sugar white beaches. He is probably sitting in the cockpit of his sailboat with his beloved wife holding hands, saying nothing, for words are not necessary. The old sailor then glances out the window at the snow and then falls into a deep sleep.

The old sailor has a magnificent dream. In his dream he is on a sailing voyage, unlike any ever before or will ever be again. This dream is so real that the old sailor can smell the pungent odor of the sea. He can feel the tug of the tiller in his hand and the wind on his face. He sees things that defy reality. Then his head nods down, and he suddenly awakens.

The old sailor walks to the window to look at the snow and suddenly sees and hears something that is unbelievable, and even magical. The old sailor at first believes that what he sees is real. Then he decides he must be practical and it must be just a dream, or at least he tries to convince himself that is all it is—a dream, just a dream, but is it?

I believe the real story behind this poem is unwritten. I can see the old sailor waking-up, but still half asleep, and when he looks out the window the magic of his "dream" was just as real as this book you are reading. But, the old sailor could not accept the fact that he was witnessing something very special, mystical, and magical. No, after all we are not children. We have to be practical, don't we? We can't dream too big, can we? At that moment when doubt entered his mind, his dream faded away—gone forever.

You see, this poem is really not about fireflies, moonbeams, or a flying boat. These things and others in the poem represent my dreams and your dreams—all the dreams we have or once had, that people said were too big to come true. They are the dreams that people laugh at or make fun of when we tell them to other people. I think they do this because they have given up on their own dreams. So they inevitably do what was done to them. They plant that seed of doubt in the minds of the dreamer, and once that seed is planted how fast it grows. Then, when that seed matures, the dream dies forever.

The last line in the poem says "Yes, it was just a dream . . . just a dream . . . I wonder?" I think this is what happens with many of our dreams. They would, and could come true, if we found it in our hearts to keep believing in them. However, as soon as we start to have doubts about our dreams, they just fade away leaving us to wonder—what if?

Please, for your reading pleasure, enjoy—"The Dream?"

*An old sailor falls asleep in front of his fireplace on a cold snowy evening.
He has a strange dream about sailing—or was it a dream after all?*

THE DREAM?

I sat in my chair in front of the fire,
At peace with the world in my evening attire.
The only light seen was from the fireplace.
The warmth of which bathed my face.

I glanced out the window, from the sky fell snow.
Large flakes drifting down, ever so slow.
The calm was total, the world was white.
As if feathers from angel wings, were falling that night.

A rising sun suddenly started to glow.
And on the horizon was a beautiful rainbow.
I was on my boat. A warm breeze filled the sails.
I heard sounds of the sea, with its' aquatic smells.

The sea was calm. I never saw it so blue.
With colors so vivid, I can't describe them to you.
Things looked the same, except better than before.
As if God invented colors, just for me to adore.

Brightly colored birds filled the sky.
Strange beautiful fish also swam by.
The beasts of the sea and fowl of the air,
All lived in harmony, none were scared.

With tiller in hand my boat balanced just right,
I sailed through the day and into the night.
Although now night, it's strange to say,
The colors were as bright, as they were that day.

The stars twinkled like lights on a Christmas tree,
All different colors they were a sight to see.
The moon was shining, bright and full,
It was as if I was sailing, in a world without rules.

I continued to sail in this enchanted land.
Then suddenly it happened so marvelous and grand.
The moon flashed gold, and my boat rocked.
The flash was a moonbeam that my boat caught.

I looked at my sails that were worn and old.
In an instant they were new, shining like gold!
My boat began to glow before my very eyes,
The spray from the bow became a million fireflies.

With the splash of each wave, the firefly numbers grew.
They began to circle my boat, and the next thing I knew,
The glow of my boat became more than I could bear.
Too beautiful to look at, yet I couldn't help but stare.

The fireflies circled my boat faster and faster!
Their wings produced a wind and a sound like laughter.
The wind filled my sails and my boat took off.
My boat left the water, and I was aloft.

Beneath me I looked, and couldn't believe my eyes.
Sailing not on blue water, but on clouds of fireflies.
The next thing I knew, my head nodded down.
I opened my eyes, and looked all around.

The fire in the fireplace flickered orange and red.
I thought to myself, it's time for bed.
As I stretched I thought—what a strange dream!
I arose from my chair, how real it all seemed.

I walked to the window to look at the snow.
And noticed my boatshed, had the strangest glow.
Through the cracks in the shed I saw rays of gold light.
And faint laughter could be heard in the calm of the night.

I thought of the laughter the fireflies made,
And the glow of the moonbeam that carried me away.
It had to be a dream, this I know.
I looked again at the shed, but gone was the glow.

Fainter and fainter grew the laughter,
Soon it was gone, but immediately after
I thought was this real, or a dream in slumber?
Yes, it was just a dream . . . just a dream . . . I wonder?

       Cleon McClain

Cleon and Glenda with the *Glenda Kay*—2003

CH. 3

Commentary on "Old Man in a Rocking Chair"

"Old Man in a Rocking Chair" is a poem that many older sailors who have sailed since youth will be able relate to. I started thinking about writing this poem when I was reading *Beyond the West Horizon* by Eric C. Hiscock. I have read this book several times throughout my life and it is one of my favorite books in my sailing library. The last time I read it before writing "Old Man in a Rocking Chair," I realized how my perception of the book has changed as I have aged.

I remember the first time I read the book. I was a young man in my sophomore year of college. This book, more than any other, captured my imagination and sparked my interest in sailing. As I read, I was captivated by the exploits of Eric Hiscock and his wife as they sailed their boat *Wanderer III* around the world. The romance and adventure of it all was forever etched in my mind. The pictures of the exotic islands they visited with their boat in the background, caused me to daydream of the time I would visit those same islands in my own sailboat. Yes, at that time in my life, my thoughts and dreams were all in the future tense. The world was out there, just waiting for me to explore.

Forty years have passed since I first read *Beyond the West Horizon*. Now, I read it with a since of nostalgia. No, I never sailed around the world in a sailboat. Somehow living life just got in the way of that dream. I have seen many of the same places I read about in the book, only I've seen them from the deck of a cruise ship, instead of a sailboat.

I have sailed on a cruise ship from the Mediterranean Sea to Hawaii. I have traveled through the Panama Canal twice, and walked on many of the same beaches that Eric Hiscock and his wife walked. Although the dream I had as a young man to sail around the world did not come true, I still accomplished the basic goal of that dream. That's just the way life is. Often you have to give up some dreams in order to make other dreams come true.

Sailing, never the less, has been a very enjoyable part of my life. Instead of sailing around the world, I've sailed the lakes of Oklahoma. I've experienced sailing in adverse weather, explored lake islands, enjoyed gorgeous sunsets, and much more from my own sailboat. I have been blessed and have had a wonderful life.

I'm not so old that I no longer have goals, plans, and dreams, but as I age I do find myself reminiscing more and more about the past. I think we live in a time-line that is dictated by our age. When we are young, we live for the present and dream about the future. As we become middle aged we work to provide for our families, think about the past more often, but plan for our future. As we become old we take care of our basic needs, reminisce, and long for the good-old-days when we were young. All of us are at some point in this continuum throughout our life.

This is what "Old Man in a Rocking" Chair is about, the hope and adventure of the young, and the memories and reminiscing of the old. The poem is really not so much about the conversations that occur between the young boys and the old men. No, the poem is about the cycle that is as old as life itself. It is about that life time-line we are all passing through as we travel on our own personal life journey. In this poem a young boy sails his way into manhood and into old age. As you read the poem you might have a different interpretation than I have. That's okay, just because I wrote the poem doesn't mean my interpretation is the only interpretation. This poem will speak to us all differently depending on where each of us is at on our own personal time-line. A few years from now I may very well see this poem from a whole different perspective, as I progress onward in my life journey.

As the poem begins I can see the boy enthusiastically walking down the dock, probably whistling to himself as he is looking forward to a day of sailing. He sees an old sailor sitting in a rocking chair smoking a pipe. The old man looks at the boy with a "longing stare." I think the boy brought back memories causing the old man to think of a day long ago when he was like that young boy. The old man speaks to the boy because the old man can see how much the boy loves sailing, and he wants to be a part of it. In this way the old man could somehow feel like he has had something worthwhile to contribute, because sailing was all the old man had in life. He tells the boy two important things. Both were beyond the boy's comprehension at that time, but they were truths about sailing that the old man discovered in all the years he had been at sea. He tells the boy "boats have souls," and "don't fall in love with the sea." What the old man means by boats have souls, is boats can have the ability to arouse strong feelings of attachment with sailors. This makes them more than just inanimate objects, but rather, more like a living being. They become a companion and partner for the sailor. Sailors think of their boats in the same way they would think of a lover or best friend. Why? Because, when they are at sea in the worst of storms, the sailor drops his sails. He knows that he can do nothing more than trust his boat to take care of him, with the same degree of love that he has for his boat. That's why many boats have female names, because the relationship is in many ways like the marriage between a man and a woman. Both know when the chips are down, they can count on each other for help, support, and protection.

When the boy asks the old man to explain what he means by boats have souls, the old man replies, "you're too young to know, but if you sail long enough you will understand." The old man knew the boy had to experience the need to rely on his sailboat for survival, before he could fully grasp the true relationship between a sailor and his boat.

The second thing the sailor tells the boy is "don't fall in love with the sea." The old man saw all that he gave up when he fell in love with the sea—a wife, a home, and a family. In exchange, the sailor lived a life of adventure. He saw the world, met people from many different cultures, and did things that the rest of us only read about in books. Was it worth it?—For some of us yes, but for most of us, no. The old man saw how much the boy already loved sailing and the sea, and he just wanted to let the boy know what he was getting himself into if he became a sailor. The boy then grows up, becomes a sailor, grows old, and finds himself having the same conversation years later with another boy. The cycle is now complete.

The last line in the poem is my personal favorite. The line says "For the old man in the rocking chair . . . now is me." We at some point in our life, if we are fortunate enough to live into our senior years, can relate to this line. We all have a story to tell. It might not be about sailing, but no less important. I can remember talking to my grandfather. When I was a child, I loved to listen to him tell me stories of living in Oklahoma before statehood—it was then called Indian Territory. At that time I knew I would someday become old myself, but that would be a long time away. Now I'm looking the other direction. I think how fast time is moving. Where did my youth go? What happened to that little boy listening to his grandfather tell about life in Indian Territory? In essence, "The old man in the rocking chair . . . now is me."

Please, for your reading pleasure, enjoy—"Old Man in a Rocking Chair."

A young boy is given advice from an old sailor.
Many years later it is he that gives the advice.

OLD MAN IN A ROCKING CHAIR

One spring day as I walked on the dock,
I saw an old man in a rocking chair.
I stepped on my boat that gently rocked.
The old man watched with a longing stare.

The old man spoke his voice coarse and low.
So you're a sailor, said he?
It's my life I said—he said it shows,
But be careful, don't fall in love with the sea.

His skin was weathered and his hands were chapped.
He dressed like a seaman long ago.
Don't worry mister, I said to him back
I love to sail. He said, I know.

I removed my sail cover and was checking my lines.
The old man watched as he smoked his pipe.
Boats have souls, said the man in time,
Continue to sail, you'll see I'm right.

I stopped what I was doing and asked him to explain.
Legs crossed he tapped his pipe on his shoe.
Sonny you're too young to understand, he exclaimed,
But sail long enough, you'll understand too.

Mister I said to the old man,
Mind giving me a shove from the dock?
I gave him the dock line and shook his hand.
He gave me a shove—I was off!

Many years passed and I sailed the seven seas.
The old man in the rocking chair I never forgot.
Then a boy walked by, that once was like me,
As an old man watched from the dock.

The old man sat in a rocking chair,
As the boy stepped aboard a sailboat.
The old man was weathered with gray in his hair,
Wearing tattered clothes and an old sea-coat.

The boy told the old man, I'm sailing today!
The old man smiled saying, I know.
The old man said, I've something to say.
Remember, your boat has a soul.

The boy asked the old man, did you ever sail?
The old man just smiled and winked.
Sonny said he, I've done nothing else,
Since I fell in love with the sea.

The boy then said, I don't understand.
The old man said, you will when you're old.
This is the mystery I learned as a man,
That an old man told me, long ago.

The boy looked at the old man with wonder in his eyes.
I'm not sure what you mean, said he.
The old man just nodded, saying you'll learn, by and by.
For the old man knew the boy, loved the sea.

The boy said Mister will you give me a shove?
My weathered hand pushed the boat towards the sea,
As tears from my eyes, fell to the sea that I love.
For the old man in the rocking chair . . . now, is me.

Cleon McClain

Cleon at dock-side with the *Glenda Kay*—2006

CH. 4

Commentary on "Welcome Aboard!"

When I wrote "Welcome Aboard!" I was going through a difficult time in my life. My father had passed away just a couple of years earlier, and family problems concerning my mother and brother consumed my being. I was 59 years old and I found myself spending more and more time thinking about my own mortality. For the first time in my life, I was spending more time thinking about my past than I was thinking about my future.

As is the case in many of my poems, I identify with the principle character. I could easily, in my imagination, see myself someday standing before my creator giving an account of my life. I think what I might say could easily be something similar to what the old sailor in this poem says.

When the poem begins, the old sailor is confused. I don't say why he is confused. Is he confused because he died and is suddenly in a strange place? Is it because the old sailor doesn't understand why he was taken from Earth when he had so much more he wanted to do? It could be any of a million other reasons. I have my idea as to why the old sailor is confused, but I leave it up to the readers' own imagination to come to their own conclusion.

When you read the poem, notice how the old sailor answers St. Peter when he is asked to tell about himself. As with most of us we define ourselves by what we do for a living. In this case the old sailor tells St. Peter that he is a sailor. St. Peter then, in a kind way, admonishes the old sailor. He lets the old sailor know that the time for small talk is over, and it is now time for absolute honesty. The best analogy I can give is from a situation that happened years ago to me when I was teaching. I caught a student cheating on a test. I asked the student "What are you doing?" The student did not lie, but she avoided the answer she knew I wanted by saying, "I'm taking a test." The student knew that was not what I was talking about. The old sailor had to have known when he was standing in front of the gate to heaven that St. Peter already knew he was a sailor. The student did not want to tell me that she was cheating on the test and the old sailor did not want to tell St. Peter about all the times he fell short in his faith. But, the time for reckoning now had come, and just as the student knew it was time for her to tell me the truth, the sailor knew the time for confession had come for him.

It does not matter if you are a Christian or a believer of another faith, a person's religion is very personal. To talk about all the times I betrayed the very essence of my own religion is a very difficult thing for me to do. This is why I think people of all faiths can relate to this poem. Regardless of a persons' religion, we all know we make mistakes and fall short of our core beliefs.

In my Christian faith, heaven is what we are all striving for. It is the ultimate prize. Now the old sailor is standing at the gate ready to claim his prize, but it's not that easy. Just as I can remember the student as she told me she was cheating broke down and started to cry, I also can visualize the old sailor breaking down and crying as he talks to St. Peter. How difficult it would be telling the story of how he professed to be a Christian, but also having to tell of all the times he did not live a Christian life. I then think of when I put my arms around the student and told her not to cry, that everything will be alright, so too does St. Peter as he gives comfort to the old sailor.

The older I get, I've seen more and more of my family members, loved ones, and friends pass away. I have also found that the hurt, pain, and disappointments I have experienced throughout my life are cumulative. That is to say, although I don't dwell on all the bad things said and done to me throughout my life, I still cannot forget them, and I occasionally think about them. I often say "the strongest person I know is the oldest person I know." What I mean by this, is the older a person is, the more of this "stuff"—death, hurt, and pain is experienced. In heaven all this "stuff" is over for good! That is why when St. Peter says "you're finally home from sea" he's not talking about the ocean. The sea St. Peter is talking about is sin. The old sailor will never again experience death, hurt, or pain, because he will never again experience sin. Thus, he will never again be separated from God, and for us Christians that is heaven.

I have noticed as I've traveled through life, we humans are very arrogant. We often think the whole world revolves around us. I have also noticed how we often just can't manage prosperity. We have all heard the story of a person that wins the million dollar lottery and within a short time loses all the money through bad decisions. Well, the sailor finds out that he did win the ultimate lottery, and unlike the person that lost the million dollars, the old sailor will never lose his prize of heaven. The old sailor then quickly discovers this does not make him God. The arrogance that exists on earth is totally absent in heaven. This is when the old sailor immediately falls to his knees and bows before God.

It is my understanding that the single thread that ties all the major religions of the world together is the idea that if we live our lives in the proper way, we will have a better life after we die. I believe this with all my heart. Because of this belief, the last two lines of the poem are my personal favorites. I know the last two lines in the poem will one day apply to me. "For only through death could you inherit all this. Welcome Aboard—my friend." What comforting words. Death is not an ending, but rather a beginning.

Please, for your reading pleasure, enjoy—"Welcome Aboard!"

An old sailor finally meets the Captain.

WELCOME ABOARD!

An old sailor was confused,
Standing in front of the gate.
Guarded by a man who asked,
May I help you mate?

The old sailor just stared,
Silent—not saying a word.
The guard at the gate then said,
We've been expecting you sir.

Of the purest gold,
Was this gate made.
With millions of pearls,
Beautifully inlaid.

Like a mirror it shined.
You could see your reflection.
The guard then said Sir,
Are you ready for inspection?

The old sailor replied,
What be your name?
Peter, he answered.
We're so glad you came.

The old sailor's name,
From the book of life Peter read.
I'd love to hear your story,
Peter smiled and then said.

The old sailor said matey,
Sailing is what I did.
Peter said, I know,
But tell me how you lived.

Well, said the old sailor,
Captain they called me.
But my Captain was the man,
That they nailed to a tree.

On a true course always,
I tried to sail my boat.
But I often veered,
When I lost faith and hope.

But my Captain was always there,
Ready to take care of me.
And helped me back on course,
So that I could sail the sea.

On the tiller I always tried,
To keep a steady hand.
But sometimes I let go,
I think you understand.

More than once I fell,
Overboard into the sea.
That's when my Captain took,
The helm and rescued me.

There were times I got in trouble,
When I read my compass wrong.
Often I was weak,
But my Captain was always strong.

Many times I sinned,
But one thing I did right.
I stayed close to my Captain,
And never left his sight.

Peter said, that is why,
You are standing here today.
Although you're not perfect,
He loves you anyway.

Soon I'll open the gate,
So that you can come inside.
You will then be with Captain,
Forever, Peter replied.

Behind the gate you will find,
Your loved ones all will be.
Together you will be forever,
You're finally home from sea.

No more tears, no more pain,
Will you ever know.
For if this was not true,
The Captain would tell you so.

The angel Gabriel then appeared,
Dressed in dazzling white.
With golden trumpet in his hand,
He blew with all his might.

The voice of the Captain,
Was heard as a mighty wind.
It is time to let my good,
And faithful servant in.

The sound of Gabriel's trumpet,
Through heaven echoed loud.
The old sailor then,
Fell to his knees and bowed.

The Captain then commanded,
St. Peter, Open the gate!
His voice was like thunder,
And all of heaven did shake.

The pearly gate began to open,
The sailor could hear angels singing.
The sailor finally saw the Captain,
A million bells began ringing.

St. Peter said to the old sailor,
Aren't you glad your old life came to an end?
For only through death could you inherit all this.
Welcome aboard!—my friend.

                          Cleon McClain

CH. 5

Commentary on "The Lady Mae"

I have owned four sailboats in my life. Three of the four were older used boats, and one was sparkling new, purchased off the showroom floor at a boat show. I have also owned a number of powerboats, and currently own a small powerboat as well as a small sailboat. I can't explain it other than to say, I have developed an affection for my sailboats that I never did for my powerboats. This is because a powerboat is a machine not unlike my car. I simply start it up and drive it across the water. A sailboat on the other hand, requires a relationship between the captain, crew, sailboat, water, and wind to accomplish the same task. As with any relationship, not all the participants are willing to cooperate all the time. Sometimes the wind is too strong or too weak. The water may have an unfavorable current. The sails may need attention and so on.

It is this "relationship" that a person either loves or hates. I have heard many people say they do not like sailing because it's boring. Well, sailing is boring for those people because they have not fallen in love with this "relationship." My love for this "relationship" is why I can sit in my sailboat becalmed, not moving for hours and still not be bored to death. People that are not sailors just cannot understand this. I explain it like this. We humans can sit with someone we truly love for hours just holding hands, saying very little and not be bored. Why? Because of the relationship we have with the person we are holding hands with. That's the kind of relationship we sailors have with our sailboats and sailing. I know this may sound strange, but that is the best way I can describe it. My wife can attest to this fact. She has watched me for hours tinkering with, or just sitting in my sailboat, while it was on the trailer under the carport. Often, I am thinking about how I can renovate or improve the performance of my sailboat. I must however, admit that this is often where I do some of my best daydreaming.

Another thing I have noticed is the affection I have for my old used sailboats is much greater than that for the new sailboat I once owned. I have pictures of all the used sailboats I have owned, but not a single picture of the sailboat I purchased new. The sailboat I now own is 37 years old and I have had it for nine years. I have put far more money into the boat than it is worth and I find this is common for many sailboat owners. I've heard it said that the two best days in the life of a boat owner are the day you buy the boat and the day you sell it. This might have been true for the sailboat I bought new, but never for my used sailboats. That brings me to my next point.

The reason I had a closer "relationship" with my used sailboats is because I had to spend so much time working on them. It is during this time I truly came to love these boats. The new boat was prettier and had that new boat smell that we all love, but I never spent that quality time developing that "relationship."

Old boats also develop character over time. You might even call it a personality. Those dings and scars they pick-up are like gray hair in people. They show maturity and give you a since of security that they have stood the test of time. There is a story behind each one of those dings and scars. If boats could only talk- what stories they could tell!

I have never purchased a boat in which the previous owner kept a log. I would have loved to have read of the adventures that produced those scars on my old boats. I must also admit I have never kept a log myself, but I have written several short stories of some of the adventures and misadventures I've had in my current boat (some of which are found in the appendices of this book). I will see that whoever I eventually sell my boat to gets these stories. Maybe they will appreciate some of the dings and scars I've added to my present boat.

All the above is what I was thinking about when I wrote the poem "The Lady Mae". A young man is very much caught up in the excitement of buying a brand new sailboat. He suddenly sees an old dilapidated sailboat with weeds and vines growing all over it. The old rotting boat is lying on its side in a field away from all the new sailboats. After deciding upon which new sailboat to buy, out of curiosity, he walks over to the old dilapidated boat to take a look. His first reaction is the old boat is simply ready for the bone yard. The man however, does not just walk away and start looking at the new boat he is going to buy. No, he spends some time with the old boat. I can see him walking around it, maybe even kicking the side of the old boat much like a person might kick the tires of a car they are thinking about buying. Then something draws him to dip the water out of the cockpit of the old boat, probably with an old can he sees lying on the ground close to the boat. The man more than likely doesn't know why, but for some reason he crawls into the old moldy cabin, wiping away a bunch of old cobwebs. Then suddenly as he is exploring the inside of the cabin, he finds something that makes this boat very special. At that moment he falls in love with this broken down shell of a boat, and in his eyes it then becomes the most beautiful boat in the entire boatyard.

When I look at my old sailboat with her faded paint and all her imperfections, I see what the man in the poem sees—the most beautiful sailboat in the world.

Please, for your reading pleasure, enjoy—"The Lady Mae."

A man at a boatyard in the process of choosing a new boat to buy sees something in a field that changes his mind.

THE LADY MAE

I walked through a boatyard one summer day,
Looking at all the bright shiny boats.
Tall aluminum masts with halyards clinging away,
All made of fiberglass with glossy gel-coats.

In the air was the smell that all new boats have,
That makes owning a new boat a must.
It's a smell that's not good, but not really bad.
Yet oh, how it makes my heart lust.

As my eyes scanned the boatyard, deciding which boat to buy,
I noticed something in a field covered with vines.
I looked back at the yard, and what did I spy,
But a shiny new sailboat, soon to be mine.

My new boat picked out, I looked back at the field,
Curious about what was under those vines.
As I walked towards the object, wondering what it would yield,
Little did I know what I would find.

Under the vines lay an old wooden boat,
I could tell it had been there for years.
Lying on its side, gone was all hope,
For the end of it's life, was near.

It's cockpit was filled with dirty water,
The cabin covered with mildew and mold.
To save this old boat would be too much bother,
For the wooden boat was just, too old.

The water in the cockpit had to be dipped out,
But the inside of the cabin looked dry.
I crawled into the cabin to look about,
And what do you think caught my eye?

In a bin under a bunk, I found a leather book.
Old with yellowed pages and mold on the cover.
I wiped it off, and thought I'd take a look.
Little did I know, what I had discovered.

The book was the log of the *Lady Mae*.
The name of the boat I had found.
I could tell she was quite-a-boat in her day,
But now she lay rotting, on the ground.

The *Lady Mae* was over a hundred years old,
Built in England in the year 1903.
When World War I came—so the log told,
The *Lady Mae* had to set out to sea.

Across the Atlantic to the U.S. she sailed,
On a top secret mission that changed history.
We would lose the war if the *Lady Mae* failed,
But the rest of the story remains a mystery.

At this point in the log, three pages were torn out.
The log then tells only of sailing Chesapeake Bay.
We'll never know what the secret mission was about,
Except the war was won, because of the *Lady Mae*.

Inside the log I found a neatly folded note.
Carefully I opened it to see what it said.
From the President of the United States who wrote,
America thanks the *Lady Mae*—it read.

I closed the log and took a good look at the boat.
Somehow she now looked different to me.
With love and work, I could again make her float,
And once again, she would sail the sea.

I crawled out of the *Lady Mae and* onto the ground,
With the log in my hand I walked away.
The smell of the new boats that were scattered all around,
Just didn't seem the same, as earlier that day.

A salesman asked, "Have you had enough time?
Which boat would you like to buy today?"
I pointed across the field, towards the vines,
And said, "Put a SOLD sign, on the *Lady Mae*."

       Cleon McClain

Cleon with his Columbia 22—1978

CH. 6

Commentary on "The Mouse!"

My best friend Jerry MacLean, my wife Glenda, and I were walking on a dock in Dubrovnik, Croatia while we were on a Mediterranean cruise. We were talking about the events of the day. At one point our conversation turned to a short discussion about the rat guards on the ships dock-lines. For those who are unfamiliar with rat guards, they are large circular metal disks that are placed on the dock-lines, to prevent rats from crawling up the lines and boarding the ship. It was a short conversation, but later that evening while I was lying in my state room I began thinking about the possibility of a rat on a sailboat as a theme for a poem. I continued to roll this idea around in my head for two or three months until the idea crystallized and I began writing the poem "The Mouse!"

Rodents can pose serious problems aboard boats. They can contaminate the food and water, as well as cause tremendous damage to the equipment, especially to electrical wiring and electronics. On small sailboats making an ocean passage, this can be a life threatening event. Small boat sailors, in particular blue water sailors, understand this and are forever vigilant for the first signs of a rodent.

From the very beginning, I decided to make the poem "The Mouse!" a light-hearted poem. As I have mentioned rodents on boats are serious, but the reactions of people to rodents are often humorous. If you want to see a 200 pound man jump up on a chair, just let a little mouse run under his feet!

Originally, I intended the poem to be about a blue water sailor who was making a Pacific crossing. Throughout the crossing, the sailor was going to have one misadventure after another as he battled a mouse that was aboard his small sailboat. Then when he finally makes landfall, the sailor was going to be so frustrated that he sells his boat to get rid of the mouse.

When I started to compose the poem my story-line turned a different direction. The basic theme remained as I originally planned with some modifications. The light-hearted nature of the poem also remained in tack, but I started to notice that woven in this light-heartiness was actually a metaphor with a serious message. It became a poem that speaks of our human emotions and frailties through humor. A poem about how we so often allow anger, obsession, and paranoia to destroy our lives.

The sailor in "The Mouse!" allowed his obsession for this little mouse to become so great that he not only hurts himself, but also destroys the thing he loves most—his boat. This "boat" in our lives might be a spouse, our children, a loved one, our health, or whatever it is you love most of all. How often do we let the "mouse" in our life cause us to hurt ourselves or our loved ones? How many of us destroy our health and families by drinking, or using drugs, or allowing our work to come between us and our families? The "mouse" could be a bad temper, money, jealousy, prejudice, bigotry and the list could go on and on. Yes, we all have a "mouse" in our lives that we need to learn to control so we don't end up like the sailor in the poem sinking our own "boat"!

As in most tragedies, the story doesn't end with just the destruction of his boat. No, although the sailor finally gets rid of the mouse, he will never truly be free from that mouse. The "mouse" is always in his mind. He can never forget the mouse or forget how that mouse caused him to make such a bad decision as to sink his own boat. That mouse changed the sailor forever. At the end of the poem the sailor has become so paranoid that he is no longer rational. The "mouse" in the sailor's head is now much worse than the mouse ever was on his boat.

This poem has a moral. Be careful of the "mouse" you allow on your "boat" for it can destroy your life. I hope as you read "The Mouse!" it's absurdities makes you laugh, while the tragedy and implications makes you think, and just maybe this poem will help each of us to re-evaluate the "mouse" we all have in our "boat".

Please, for your reading pleasure, enjoy—"The Mouse!"

*A sailor's life is forever changed when he finds
a mouse onboard his small sailboat.*

THE MOUSE!

This is a story that will make you cry.
It's the absolute truth, but I wish it was a lie.
It's about a mouse, that was on my small yacht.
He ruined my life. I kid you not!

I remember when that monster, first caught my eye.
Running over the handrail to the cabin inside.
It looked cute and innocent, as it ran into a hole.
But it really was a devil, out to destroy my soul.

I tied-off the tiller and went into the cabin.
Things got ugly. You won't believe what happened!
Cooking oil was dripping from a storage bin.
That rodent chewed a hole, in the bottle within.

I opened the bin door and the bottle fell out.
Oil spilled on the floor splattering all about.
I slipped on the oil, feet over my head.
I landed on my back. I thought I was dead.

All the contents began to fall from the bin.
When a sack of flour, hit me square on the chin.
The sack exploded, a white cloud filled the air.
The cabin was a mess with flour everywhere.

I jumped to my feet. My eyes seeing red.
When on the open bin door, I hit my head.
I fell to my knees. Pain went from head to toe.
I had knocked myself out, and bloodied my nose!

I don't know how long it was before I came-to.
But there I was laying in all that muck and goo.
On the floor where I lay in all that flour and oil,
My nose still bleeding, my blood starting to boil.

There in my face stared two beady eyes.
I was a broken man. I started to cry.
That horrible mouse just an inch from my face!
Where was my pride? I was a disgrace.

I jumped to my feet. The mouse started to run.
He ran in the hole. I got my gun.
I stuck the barrel of my gun in the hole.
I cocked the trigger, and let it go!

The gun went off. I blew a hole in my yacht!
But this was a war that had to be fought.
My boat began to sink. Water was up to my head.
But that was okay, for that monster was dead.

I could see the shore and I started to swim.
When floating on a cracker box I suddenly saw HIM!
He was floating towards shore, and not even wet.
The worst day of my life, was the day that we met.

Some think I'm paranoid, but that's not true.
I'm looking for that monster. You would be too!
I know he's out there, so I'm watching my back.
It's just a matter of time, before again he attacks.

I am now sailing a brand new boat.
I'm going to make sure that it stays afloat.
The next time that devil boards my boat to attack.
He'll find in the cabin, I set a thousand mouse traps.

Cleon McClain

Glenda sailing the *Glenda Kay*—2004

CH. 7

Commentary on "Autumn Evening"

Some of the most memorable times I have had with my sailboat were not actually sailing at all. In fact, I have many fond memories about sailing that did not occur while I was even on my sailboat. A good example of this happened to me just yesterday when I was looking at a picture of my mother and me sailing on my first sailboat. Memories started to flood into my mind. Although the picture was almost forty years old and of very poor quality, the memories of my mother and that old boat were crystal clear.

The sailboat was called a Seagull and very small—far too small to ever spend the night on. I thought about the evenings I spent at my parents' one-room cabin. My family and friends were always there. We would eat hamburgers, pork-n-beans, and potato salad, while we talked about the day's events. Inevitably, our conversation would turn towards talking about sailing my old sailboat, or some other water sport we were involved in during the day. I was the only person that was deeply involved in sailing, but the discussions we had were important to me then, and I cherish them even more now. I have been so blessed to have lived those moments.

Those days are now long gone, as well as many of my family and friends that are in those memories. All my aunts and uncles, as well as my father have passed away. My mother is now elderly, very frail, and in a nursing home with Alzheimer's. That horrible disease has erased most of these memories from her mind.

As I get older, my memories have become more and more precious to me. I have acquired so many good memories throughout my life that it is impossible to say which ones are the best. However, the memories I have of sailing are certainly at the top of the list. Some are memories of actually sailing, others as I have mentioned, are simply conversations about sailing—and then, there are those memories of the evenings I spent on board my sailboats. Yes, the memories I have of the evenings spent in the tiny cockpit of my sailboats are very special indeed.

Some of these special memories include the most gorgeous sunrises and sunsets I have ever seen. They have been absolutely breath taking. Many times I have watched the morning fog escape from the water into the air like gnarly fingers reaching to the sky. I remember one night my brother and friend spent the night on board. I woke-up and just looked around the cabin. I could see them sleeping in their bunks and hear the water gently lapping against the side of the boat. Everything just seemed so right with the world. I could go on and on. These memories often seem worlds away, but then, at times they seem like they occurred just yesterday.

Memories such as these are what inspired me to write the poem "Autumn Evening". All the events in the poem actually happened to me at one time or another, as I spent evenings in the cockpit of my sailboat. I hope as you read "Autumn Evening" you too will be able to see and hear in your imagination all those things I see and hear so clearly in my memory—the caws of distant crows, the sight of a magnificent sunset, the mirror reflection of beautiful fall foliage on a placid lake, being startled by some deer as they get a drink of water from the lake, and much more.

This is a poem to be read slowly in a quiet room in front of a fireplace, or maybe as you watch a sunset in a park. It's one of my favorites because of all the memories it holds for me. I hope it becomes one of your favorites too. So now, get ready to experience an evening that could never be forgotten.

Please, for your reading pleasure, enjoy—"Autumn Evening."

*A Sailor discovers the beauty of an autumn evening
from the cockpit of a small sailboat.*

AUTUMN EVENING

The sun was falling into the western sky,
When I found a cove that looked just right.
Running across the water a duck started to fly,
As I dropped anchor preparing for night.

My boat curtsied as the hook found bottom.
My sails then stowed and put to bed.
The air was crisp for it was now autumn.
I slipped on a coat and put a cap on my head.

On my one-burner stove a pan of water I did put.
A hot cup of tea would taste good to drink.
I opened a can of stew that I would later cook,
And sat in the cockpit, and began to think.

The beauty of my surroundings did my thoughts turn.
Red orange and gold was the color of the trees,
With patches of green produced by the ferns.
A kaleidoscope of color as far as I could see.

A breeze I could hear whispering through the leaves,
And the sun would soon be giving up its light.
On the lake the mirror image of the autumn trees,
Was kissing the shoreline a fond good-night.

The water now hot I sipped a cup of tea,
The stew now warming in the pot.
I continued to admire all that I could see,
And once again alone, with my thoughts.

The color of fire the sky then did become.
In the distance I could hear some crows caw.
Of all the sunsets this had to be the one,
That by far was the prettiest of them all.

Sipping my tea I almost dropped my cup,
When suddenly a noise I did hear.
Walking on the shore I saw a doe and a buck.
How surprised I was seeing the two deer.

The deer then paused to drink water from the lake.
Then quietly raised their heads and stood still.
Looking straight at my boat not a sound did they make,
Then quickly turned, and disappeared up the hill.

I finished my stew as the sky turned black.
One by one the stars started to shine.
I lay in the cockpit of my boat on my back,
Gazing at the stars for the longest time.

I heard the croak of a frog, near the shore.
Unusual for this time of year.
Although he sang solo, a mournful score,
His deep voice was music to my ears.

A million stars that night seemed to fill the sky.
What a beautiful way to end the day.
A falling star above the lake did fly,
That left a trail that slowly faded away.

My eyelids became heavy. It was time for bed.
The air became colder and had a bite.
I crawled into the cabin and looked to heaven and said,
Thank you for this autumn evening—good night.

          Cleon McClain

Cleon and his Mother sailing his first sailboat - 1973

CH. 8

Commentary on "A Boat Without a Name"

I started thinking about the poem "A Boat Without a Name" about a year before I actually put pen to paper to compose the poem. The original idea I had of the poem was much different than the final copy. Originally, I had in my mind to write a poem about several boats in a marina talking to each other. Each boat was going to tell of a personal sailing experience that had happened to them. I even started a poem with this in mind, but the poem just seemed to die before I could get beyond a few stanzas.

It was at this time I was reading through the Gospels (the first four books of the New Testament) and I noticed how often boats were mentioned, and how important they were in the ministry of Jesus. It then came to me how this was the story I really needed to tell through a poem. I thought to myself. If the boats that carried Jesus and his disciples could speak—what stories they could tell! I then decided to change my original idea just slightly. This time the boats talking to each other would be the boats that carried Jesus and his disciples. Again, I started writing the poem, and again, the poem just didn't seem to work for me. I just did not like the back and forth conversations between the boats. I then came up with the idea of having Jesus and the disciples sailing only one boat. This would simplify and add congruency to the poem. I thought about this for a couple of weeks, while I tied up some loose ends on another poem I was working on. Then, finally on my third attempt all the pieces just seemed to fall into place. Four days later "A Boat Without a Name" was completed.

Many people don't realize how important boats were to Jesus and his ministry. The primary means of transportation Jesus used was walking and sailing. Yes, the Bible does mention Jesus riding a colt/donkey, but boats and walking were the main source of transportation, with sailing being the faster of the two. I know it's hard for us in the days of cars and air travel to imagine that sailing would be a fast method of transportation. However, in the time of Jesus, sailing was to them as flying in an airplane is to us today. It was the high tech means of travel in ancient times.

The original twelve disciples were a menagerie of people. Their professions ranged from a tax collector to a doctor. We don't know the professions of all the disciples, but we do know that at a minimum four of the twelve disciples were fishermen. Peter was even the owner of his own fishing boat. I think this was not by accident. I have no way of proving this, but I think Jesus knew that the sailing skills of these men would be a valuable asset for his ministry. These men surely would have been experts in sailing, which was considered a highly trained profession at that time.

Not a lot is known about the personality of Jesus, but we do know he would have been very charismatic. He would have been the kind of person that everyone would want to be with. In my mind, I see Jesus like this—a man with a continual smile on his face and a wonderful since of humor. I see him as a very happy man that laughed a lot and enjoyed the hearing and the telling of a good joke. He was also a man with a very serious side, a good listener, and a man that thought before he spoke. Jesus was a man that had the ability to see things not as they appear, but as they really are. He was a man filled with love and void of hate. Jesus could truly forgive and forget, and forgive some more. At least this is the kind of man I think Jesus was.

I think the disciples on the other hand, were more like most of us. Jesus however, saw great potential in them. Jesus knew it would be up to them to carry-on his work after his death, and being with Jesus, made the disciples much more than they otherwise could have ever been. Jesus brought a meaning into their lives and gave them a purpose far beyond that of their chosen profession. Indeed, Jesus became not only their focus in life, but their reason for life. We Christians understand this even today. I cannot imagine how it must have felt to have actually been in Jesus's inner circle, and to have walked and talked with him the way the disciples did.

In my imagination, I can see Jesus with the disciples walking down a road or on a beach, throwing rocks in the water, laughing, and teasing each other, just like a group of young men might today. I can also see Jesus with a smile on his face as the disciples trembled with fear while in a terrible storm at sea; or the disciples standing in awe as they watch Jesus perform miracle after miracle. I can visualize them crying as Jesus tells them he will be going away and how he will be crucified. Yes, I think Jesus and the disciples had all the emotions we have today, for we humans really haven't changed that much throughout the centuries.

I try to capture some of these personalities in my poem. For instance, when Jesus first meets Peter and tells him to go back out fishing and he will catch a lot of fish. Peter goes back out and catches so many fish that he almost sinks his boat! In my poem Jesus smiles then winks and says "I told you the fish were there." I can see Jesus with his since of humor laughing like it was a practical joke, while also making a serious point. That point being, if you follow me you ain't seen nothin yet!

Another example of me trying to capture the personalities of Jesus and the disciples is found at the end of my poem. Jesus had been crucified and the disciples go fishing. Jesus then appears on the shore. Can you imagine seeing someone you loved who had died and you never thought you would see again, suddenly standing in front of you? The joy you would feel would be indescribable. That is the kind of joy I've tried to capture in that part of my poem. I have done my best to incorporate these kinds of emotions in several places in the poem. I wanted to do more than just tell Bible stories. I wanted to try to make the stories come alive. I hope I've succeeded.

I have added side notes in the left hand margin to tell where each story in the poem can be found in the Bible. Most of the stories in this poem are told in more than one book of the Bible. I simply placed the side note of the account of the stories that I used when I wrote the poem. It is my hope that these side notes will be beneficial to anyone that would like to read the stories themselves from the Bible. I should say at this point that I used the New Living Translation and there may be a small variation within the stories, depending on what translation you read. Also, this poem, as well as my commentary, is strictly my thoughts and poetic interpretation of these biblical events. I hope my poem and commentary will be read and enjoyed in this context.

Although the stories in this poem are from the Bible, I don't think my friends of other faiths will find anything offensive, and it is my hope that all will enjoy reading—"A Boat Without a Name". Now get ready to sail the Sea of Galilee and go fishing with the fishers of men.

Please, for your reading pleasure, enjoy—"A Boat Without a Name."

A fishing boat tells his story about Jesus.

A BOAT WITHOUT A NAME

I am just a fishing boat.
I never had a name.
Although I am not famous,
I made history just the same.

My story that I will tell you,
Started early one spring day.
A man that they called Jesus,
Just happened to walk my way.

Luke 5: 1-11

All night I had been working,
Sailing the Sea of Galilee.
On board me were the fishermen,
Who were just as tired as me.

The fishermen were now busy,
Working at cleaning their nets.
I was resting at water's edge,
When Jesus jumped on my deck.

There was a crowd of people,
As always following Him.
He spoke strange words, I never heard,
From my deck to them.

They listened very intently,
To His every word.
The way He spoke of love and peace,
Was something never heard.

Jesus told the fishermen,
That He would like some food.
We've fished all night my Master,
Tell us what we can do.

We've just come in from fishing,
And did not catch a fish.
But we will drop our net again,
If that is what you wish.

Jesus said in deeper water,
This time drop your net.
If you will have a little faith,
Lots of fish you'll catch.

The fishermen then boarded me.
Once again I set sail.
A peace came over all of us.
We knew we could not fail.

We caught so many fish.
I thought that I would sink.
They sailed me back to the shore.
Jesus just smiled and winked.

I told you the fish were there.
They were always in the sea.
But you'll become fishers of men,
If you will follow me.

Mark 4:35 - 41 The next time that they boarded me,
I sailed to the other side.
Of the Sea of Galilee,
When a storm hit by surprise.

It was the worst I've ever seen.
I was taking on water fast.
Waves were breaking over my rail,
I did not have long to last.

These men were called disciples now.
Many had sailed for years.
But they could not save me now.
They were petrified with fear!

Jesus was lying at my stern,
And quietly sleeping sound.
The disciples quickly woke Him,
Saying Master we're going to drown.

Jesus shook his head and smiled.
Saying children you must be brave.
For if you had a little faith.
You would not be afraid.

Jesus stood and said to the storm,
SILENCE! with stretched out arms.
The storm was calmed and Jesus said,
I'll keep you all from harm.

Jesus smiled and lay back down,
And fell asleep right away.
The disciples said, who is this man,
That the wind and sea obey?

They bailed the water from my bilge,
I peacefully sailed all night.
Arriving at a distant shore,
As people cheered with delight.

Matthew 14: 14-21

Once again from my deck,
To a multitude Jesus spoke.
The people listened to His words,
That gave them cause for hope.

Jesus then jumped from my deck.
Through the crowd He then walked.
All the sick were instantly healed,
Of love He always talked.

Over five-thousand were in the crowd,
They were hungry and without food.
Only five loaves and two fish do we have,
Jesus, what will we do?

Feed my people Jesus said,
My Father will provide.
All were fed, a miracle they said,
Where's your faith? Jesus replied.

Matthew 14: 22-33   The disciples then boarded me,
Leaving Jesus and people behind.
Jesus said he'd see them soon,
At the appropriate time.

The disciples sailed me out to sea.
The sun gave up its' light.
Darkness fell with an eerie spell.
Something would happen tonight.

The wind and waves grew higher.
The disciples were stricken with fear.
I was sure I was going to sink.
The end would soon be here.

Early morning about three o'clock,
A ghost on the water was walking.
Fear not take courage, said the ghost,
But no!—It was Jesus talking.

A disciple who they call Peter,
Said Master is it really you?
If it is let me walk on water,
And prove what you say is true.

Jesus held out his hand and said,
Come walk to me my child.
Peter stepped into the water,
And walked towards Jesus's smile.

The storm was growing stronger,
From Jesus, Peter looked away.
Peter then started sinking,
Yelling save me Jesus, I pray!

Jesus then grabbed Peter,
And said together we'll walk to the boat.
Jesus then told Peter,
When you doubt you also lose hope.

The storm immediately ended,
On water they walked towards me.
Peter climbed on board with Jesus,
Who saved him from the sea.

They praised Jesus from my deck,
And told him they loved him so.
They called him the Son of God.
Saying this we all now know.

John 21: 1-14

The last time I saw Jesus,
The disciples were fishing on me.
I heard them say that Jesus,
Was crucified—nailed to a tree.

We had been fishing the entire night,
And the sun was starting to rise.
A man then yelled how's fishing?
No good, the disciples replied.

On the starboard side drop your net.
The man on the beach did cry.
We dropped the net, it filled with fish.
It was Jesus not dead—but alive!

Peter was so excited.
Jumping overboard to Jesus he swam.
Laughing and waving they pulled in the fish.
But holes, were in Jesus's hands.

The disciples sailed me to the shore.
They laughed and hugged each other.
He built a fire to cook the fish.
They called each other brother.

I watched them eat around the fire.
I could not hear what they said.
Sometimes laughing, sometimes crying,
While they ate their fish and bread.

That was the last time I saw Jesus,
But I heard the disciples talk.
They said He died and took their sins,
With Him on the cross.

He was the son of a carpenter,
But I know He spent time at sea.
I'm just a boat without a name,
But Jesus was Captain to me.

Cleon McClain

CH. 9

Commentary on "The Treasure"

I remember when I was a child my brother and I spent much of our time pretending. An old broom stick could be a sword. Blocks of wood nailed together were ships. Popsicle sticks were cars, and an old towel tied around our neck made us superman. I think pretending is a very important part in the development of a child. It is through pretending that children develop their imagination.

I spend a lot of time talking about imagination in my commentaries. Maybe it's because without using my imagination I would not be able to write most of my poems. So imagination is critical to do what I do. I can't imagine how dull life would be without it. Often I wonder if we are doing our children a disservice these days by giving them too much.

In this high-tech computer driven age, our children needs very little imagination for them to entertain themselves. They no longer need to use blocks of wood to pretend they are driving a boat. They just turn on an electronic gadget and instantly the boat appears on a monitor. Then, if they do not have those electronic games to play with, they are bored. If you would hand children a Popsicle stick or a block of wood to replace that electronic device, they would look at you like you're crazy, and ask what you expect them to do with this? I don't stay up at night worrying about this, but I do occasionally think about how simple things use to be.

"The Treasure" is a poem about those simpler times. Back in the days that I can remember when marbles, yo-yo's, and the old tops that were thrown with a string were a boy's most prized possessions. In those days, play was more about pretending and less about the toys you had to play with.

In the poem "The Treasure" the Captain of a bunch of "cut-throat" pirates is faced with mutiny. The Captain survives and even finds the buried treasure. But, even the Captain has to follow the orders of his mother.

As you read the poem "The Treasure" I hope it brings back some good memories of the innocence, imagination, and love we often leave in our childhood. Yes, this poem is about the treasures we all seek, but are often so hard for us adults to find—innocence, imagination, and especially love.

Please, for your reading pleasure, enjoy—"The Treasure."

Treasure can be as close as your own backyard
if you have the imagination to look.

THE TREASURE

It was the meanest group of cut-throats that ever sailed.
I saw blood in their eyes as they looked at me.
With swords in their hands I heard one of them yell,
Make him walk the plank, and commit his body to the sea.

I was the captain of this motley crew.
They hated my guts, and wanted the treasure we've seized.
But only the treasure map, that contained the clues,
Was keeping those sea-dogs from killing me.

I pulled out my sword and looked them square in the eyes,
And told them to back-off if they wanted the loot.
For I knew the only thing that was keeping me alive,
Was the treasure map that I had, hidden in my boot.

They slowly walked towards me. I slowly backed away.
They were determined to kill me. I could see it in their face.
I had to act fast if I was to live through this day.
I then turned and ran, they immediately gave chase.

As I ran to the lifeboat, they grabbed my cloak.
I pulled away and jumped on board.
I cut the lines that were holding the boat.
We fell to the sea, free once more.

I looked up at the ship. The pirates were at the rail.
They were laughing at me as I drifted away.
Leaving me to die, they continued to sail.
The map is in his cabin. I heard someone say.

With an oar and my cloak, I then made a sail,
And with the map in my boot I would have the last laugh.
They would soon discover, that they had all failed.
They would never get the treasure, for it was mine at last.

I sailed on course, and on a sandy beach I did land.
I counted five steps from an old tree and then stopped.
I then looked on the ground, with my treasure map in hand,
And under an old log, I saw an **X** that marked the spot.

My heart in my chest was pounding hard,
Excited the treasure just inches away.
I'd survived a mutiny and traveled so far.
The treasure was mine. I'd dreamt of this day.

I lifted the treasure from the hole with care,
And gently set it on the ground.
It was mine—all mine with no one would I share,
For this treasure chest, I alone found.

A pirate's voice I heard as if from another world.
Stop playing. It's time for lunch Tommy.
It was not a pirate, for the voice came from a girl.
Pirates don't eat lunch. Can I play longer Mommy?

No! It's time to eat. Give me that box and wash your hands.
Oh! Mommy that's my treasure chest. Not just a box.
She looked in the box and suddenly understands.
For the treasures were her son's yo-yo, and a toy top.

          Cleon McClain

Cleon sailing the *Glenda Kay*—2009

CH. 10

Commentary on "A Sailor's Wife"

I have been so blessed to have a wonderful marriage. My wife and I have been inseparable for 26 years now. Yes, we have been apart for a few days at a time, but never for months, or even weeks for that matter. Glenda is more than my wife. She is my life. In fact, we were best friends for nearly ten years before we ever started dating. Maybe that is why we have such a special relationship, because we knew each other so well before we became romantically involved. She knew all my flaws (and believe me I have more than my share!) before we decided to start dating. This is the kind of relationship the man and wife has in my poem "A Sailor's Wife"—an extraordinarily close relationship with each other that only couples with that kind of love could truly understand.

I think that is why most blue water sailors that make ocean voyages in very small boats have been younger single men. I know there are exceptions to that rule. I can think of a half a dozen just off the top of my head; starting with Robert Manry who sailed his 13 ½ foot Tinkerbelle across the Atlantic in 1965 at age of 47. But like I said, these are basically the exception to the rule. I have read many accounts of these special sailors, and one thing most all of them have in common is a sense of guilt and heartache when they leave their loved ones behind. Most of them, from what I've read, understand the hardships and stress they place square on the shoulders of the people they love most. For while the sailors are living their dreams, their loved ones can only worry and pray about them. Each time the phone rings, their hearts must sink into their stomachs, wondering if this is the phone call that gives them the bad news that their husband is lost at sea. Or even worse, if weeks and months pass by with no news at all and they realize that their husband will never return—gone forever.

It is one of these special couples my poem "A Sailor's Wife" is about. A couple that loves each other more than life itself. A wife that only wants her husband to be happy, and is willing to suffer anguish beyond belief to see he lives his dream. She knows if she does not allow her husband to do this, he will always have regrets, and she loves him too much for that. She tries her best to be brave, but when the time comes for his departure she can no longer hold her feelings in. As he sails from the dock her emotions flood through her trembling body. She realizes she may be watching the only man she has ever loved, and ever could love, sail out of her life, possibly forever.

The husband has planned this voyage for years, maybe even his whole life. His eyes are wide open to the dangers that lie ahead. He doesn't even know for sure why he has this deep desire to do this. All he knows is this voyage has become more important to him than life itself. He is a man torn apart by his obsession to sail an ocean, or stay with the love of his life. As he sails away his mind is spinning in his head. He thinks about his wife and the time they spent together, as he watches her break down on the dock in grief. He tries to console her as he sails from the dock, but their grief is unimaginable.

He then thinks about the voyage that after all these years is within his grasp. He knows that this will be his only opportunity to ever live that dream. He looks back at the dock one more time and what he sees, breaks his heart. It's more than he can stand. He then looks at the ocean that lies in front of him. He has to make a decision. What does he do? Does he sail back to the love of his life? Is the love for his wife stronger than his selfish need to live a dream? Or, does he turn his back on her and continue the voyage? What would you do?

Please, for your reading pleasure, enjoy—"A Sailor's Wife."

A sailor says good-bye to his wife

A SAILOR'S Wife

This voyage I had planned,
For oh so many years,
But as I sailed away,
I only saw her tears.

They were flowing down her cheeks,
Her hands in the air,
Waving good-bye, to my wife,
Was so hard to bear.

I told my wife I'll see you soon,
On the other side.
I forced a smile and waved good-bye,
As I watched her cry.

Across the ocean I was sailing.
I would be gone for weeks.
But with my wife I had a date.
That I was going to keep.

From my boat I yelled to my wife.
Good-bye and I love you.
Her voice cracked as she replied,
You know I love you too.

As she stood on the dock,
How lonely she did seem.
She has endured oh so much,
So I could live my dream.

I thought about yesterday,
When we were on the boat.
Don't make me a widow said she,
As if it was a joke.

Now I know it was not a joke.
She was trying to be brave.
But now she's standing on the dock.
Trembling as she waves.

We held each other closely,
Last night while in bed.
So tenderly she kissed me.
Not a word was said.

She knew tomorrow I would sail,
And be gone for many weeks.
We closed our eyes and said goodnight,
But we could find no sleep.

But now that I am leaving,
The love of my life.
It feels as if some-one,
Has cut my heart out with a knife.

I have to make this voyage.
I still don't understand why.
To leave the best thing in my life.
It's hard to say good-bye.

She looked so helpless standing there.
As I sailed away.
I still could hear her crying,
But didn't know what to say.

So I yelled "I'll be alright,"
As tears welled in my eyes.
The toughest part of a voyage,
Is having to say good-bye.

I saw her collapse on the dock,
As I sailed out of sight.
I then broke down and began to cry,
And prayed she'd be alright.

What should I do I asked myself,
For oh, how my heart ached.
Should I turn back or should I sail.
A decision I had to make.

I wiped my tears and took a breath,
Then turned to face the sea.
I knew if I looked back again,
I would never leave.

The sea was now calling me,
And that call I had to heed.
I have a hunger for this voyage,
I know that I must feed.

My wife I know would understand,
And say go on and sail.
She knows how much this means to me,
And would not want me to fail.

I must go on and not look back,
And think only of tomorrow.
When we will be together again,
And gone will be our sorrow.

Before that day can ever come,
I have to cross an ocean.
Who knows what tomorrow brings.
I haven't the slightest notion.

But this I know the love I carry,
In my heart for my wife.
Will see me through this ocean voyage,
No matter what the strife.

Across the ocean I'll soon arrive.
It will be a glorious day.
On the dock I'll see my wife.
laughing as she waves.

I'll hold her in my arms,
And never let her go.
I'll kiss her lips and tell my love,
How much I love her so.

Until that day I will remember,
Her standing on the dock.
Trembling, crying, and waving good-by,
Collapsing so distraught.

It's hard to be a sailor,
And leave my love, my life.
I think it's so much harder though,
To be a sailors' wife.

      Cleon McClain

Glenda with the *Glenda Kay*—2004

CH. 11
Commentary on "This is Good—All is Well"

Each year I read the Bible from Genesis through Revelation. I say this not to brag or promote myself, or even my religion, but rather in the way of explanation as to how I came to write "This is Good—All is Well." I had completed reading the Bible early in August of 2012 and was starting to read the Bible through a second time. As I read the creation story (Genesis 1:1—2:2), I felt a need to capture this wonderful story in a very unique way. What better way than a poem? When I started writing the poem I decided I would like to use a similar style as is in the Bible, but my question was how am I going to make this happen?

The Creation story is the first story told in the Bible. Historically, Jews and Christians alike believe the Creation story, as well as the first five books of the New Testament, was written by Moses. The book of Genesis, and in particular the Creation story, is arguably the most beautiful piece of literature ever written. It divides the creation of the universe into six events called days, with a seventh event being that of God resting. Each event then ends with a repetitive statement. In my feeble attempt, I try to recapture this literary format with my poetic interpretation interjected.

The final result is my poem "This is Good—All is well" which is a poem of the Creation story with a twist. In this poem God creates the Universe and all that is in it from the cockpit of a sailboat. I wrote this poem to be a fun way to tell the Creation story and I hope it will be read and enjoyed within this context.

Although the story line of this poem is from the Bible, I don't think my friends of other faiths will find anything offensive, and it is my hope that all will enjoy reading, "This is Good—All is Well." Now get ready to take a sailing voyage that created the Universe!

Please, for your reading pleasure, enjoy—"This is Good—All is Well."

God takes a sailing voyage and creates the universe.

THIS IS GOOD—ALL IS WELL

In the beginning when God set sail,
Darkness was everywhere no light prevailed.
God then decided He needed some light.
He called the light day, and darkness He called night.

The voyage now is only one day old.
God alone knows what the future will hold.
His hand on the tiller God continued to sail.
Saying "this is good—all is well."

God then separated the ocean from sky,
And put the clouds above to slowly drift by.
He sailed under a sky that was a deep blue.
All was peaceful. All was new.

The voyage now is only two days old.
God alone knows what the future will hold.
His hand on the tiller God continued to sail.
Saying "this is good—all is well."

God then said without hesitation,
Bring forth the land with lush vegetation.
The land then rose from the ocean deep.
The smell of the plants and flowers so sweet.

The voyage now is only three days old.
God alone knows what the future will hold.
His hand on the tiller God continued to sail.
Saying "this is good—all is well."

Sailing through the day, and night that He loved,
There was no sunset or beauty above.
God gave the command and in a blink of an eye.
The sun, moon, and stars, then danced across the sky.

The voyage now is only four days old.
God alone knows what the future will hold.
His hand on the tiller God continued to sail.
Saying "this is good—all is well."

God then waved his hand, across water and sky.
Let fish fill the sea and birds begin to fly.
The music of the birds filled the air with their songs,
While schools of fish swam, as God sailed along.

The voyage now is only five days old.
God alone knows what the future will hold.
His hand on the tiller God continued to sail.
Saying "this is good—all is well."

God then sailed close to the land that he made,
Creating the animals that scurried and played.
In his own image God made boy and girl.
Be fruitful and multiply, take care of my world.

The voyage now is only six days old.
God alone knows what the future will hold.
His hand on the tiller God continued to sail.
Saying "this is good—all is well."

God then laid back in the cockpit to rest.
His work now done, the voyage a success.
He declared this day holy, and gave it his blessing.
His creation completed, it was now time for resting.

The voyage now is only seven days old.
God alone knows what the future will hold.
His hand on the tiller God continued to sail.
Saying "this is good—all is well."

The voyage continues to this very day.
God's hand on the tiller steadfast and brave.
The ship we all sail is not ours to command.
We're simply the crew God holds in his hand.

The voyage now is incredibly old.
God alone knows what the future will hold.
His hand on the tiller God continues to sail.
Saying "this is good—all is well."

Cleon McClain

CH. 12

Commentary on "The Visit"

When I was a young man in college, I developed a grand plan to sail solo around the world in a small sailboat. I had read the accounts of others that had done this and their adventures became my dream. I even bought a sailboat to make this voyage. It was a Columbia 22. The boat was not much to look at, small, and needed some modifications, but seaworthy enough for the voyage. No, the voyage never happened and my dream has always remained just a dream.

I think the reason this dream never became a reality can be summed up in one of the lines from my poem "A Sailor's Wife." That line says. The toughest part of a voyage is having to say good-bye. Yes, to make that voyage and live my dream I would have had to say too many good-byes. I would have had to say good-bye to my loved ones and friends. I would have had to say good-bye, to my early teaching career, the materialism I had grown to love, my new car I just bought, and all the stuff I had accumulated. In short, what I learned from this experience, is if you wait too long to live your dream, that dream will always just remain a dream.

Not all people are like me. Some have the courage to grab their dream and live it. These are special people. My wife Glenda is one of these people. Glenda loved basketball, and when she was given the opportunity to play professional basketball, she took it. She postponed graduating college so she could live her dream. Glenda played four years while coaching one year for the All American Redheads, the first professional women's basketball team in America. The All American Redheads now has the largest exhibit in the Women's Basketball Hall of Fame in Knoxville Tennessee. The exhibit contains the old limousine Glenda and her team used when they were on the road, as well as several pictures of Glenda with her team. The All American Redheads were also inducted into the Naismith Basketball Hall of Fame in Springfield, Massachusetts—the only women's team to have been given that honor. After four years playing professional basketball Glenda graduated college and had a very successful career as a teacher/coach. She retired from public education after 30 years. Glenda is now a supervisor of intern teachers and instructor at Bacone College in Muskogee, Oklahoma.

I tell you these stories to make a point. There are "dreamers" and there are "achievers". I really don't think one is better than the other. They are just different. The "achievers" achieve their dreams and live the lives that help keep us "dreamers" going. They are often the rich, famous, and adventuress. They are the movie stars, singers, and professional athletes. They are the adventurers that sail around the world, climb Mt. Everest and so on. The truth is we "dreamers" are also important. While we dream our dreams we also work hard. We build the houses for people to live in. We work in the stores, teach in the school, are care givers in the hospitals, and haul the garbage. We are the police officers, firemen, plumbers, and truck drivers. Yes, we are the people that get our hands dirty, getting things done. It takes all of us to keep things going—the "achievers" to inspire, and the "dreamers" to do the work.

I think if we are honest we all know someone we secretly would like to be, if only for a day or two. That's not to say we are unhappy or disappointed with ourselves or our lives. I'm just saying it is human nature to look at someone else, and see them as having a life that is in some way beyond our lives. We see them bigger than life, and yes, we even envy them. I have come to understand that wealth, fame, and living a life of adventure does not necessarily translate into happiness. Many of the people that we think of as having the perfect life are in reality extremely unhappy. I wonder how often the rich and famous get tired of all the attention, and would love to just spend a few days walking through the streets of a town without being noticed?

At the risk of sounding cliché, happiness has to come from within. Being at peace with yourself and comfortable in your own skin is worth more than fame or fortune. I will always know people who I will look-up to and admire, but in truth, I have been blessed far more than any man deserves. Although this may not be the case for everyone, I do think this is true for most of us. It has been my experience that you don't have to look far to find someone worse off than yourself.

I have heard people say "the harder you work the luckier you become." I believe this. I also believe the better choices you make, the better your life will be. Life is a series of choices and the choices we make determine the kind of life we live. Most choices really do not matter, like what color of shirt I wear today, or what I eat for lunch. Other choices however, can change our life forever, such as: applying yourself to get the best education possible or whether or not to use drugs. You get the idea? We all know this.

I have made my share of bad choices, but I always knew where to draw that line. That line was between a bad choice and a horrible choice that could destroy my life. As a life-long educator, this is one subject that I can go off on. For the sake of this commentary, and to keep from sounding too preachy, I'll restrain myself. I'll simply say, I have seen so many wonderful, bright, and beautiful students, (who I affectionately call my kids) make some of these horrible choices, and it breaks my heart. What I do believe with all my being, is we become what we become, because of the choices we make. Thank God most of us do at least an adequate job in this regard.

All the above and more, is what "The Visit" is about. It speaks to us "achievers," and "dreamers." It tells about choices, love, envy, happiness, and family.

Uncle John comes to visit his brother and family on a three day leave from his ship. It doesn't matter the time. It could be a whaling ship of the 1700's or a nuclear submarine of today. The story is timeless. Uncle John is an "achiever" and a man's man. He is bigger-than-life both in stature and in personality. He has done everything and been everywhere.

Uncle John is the life of the party and the envy of all. The stories of his sea adventures are captivating, and in the eyes of his nephew, "little Billy," as well as his parents, Uncle John is the ultimate hero.

Uncle John's brother and sister-in-law are "dreamers" and very average. Their names are never mentioned in the poem. They could be you or me, just two hard-working people trying their best to meet the bills and raise a family. When Uncle John comes to visit, he brings with him a sense of excitement and adventure to their house that is otherwise totally absent.

Uncle John and Billy's father, like many brothers, have a deep love for each other. They were both raised by the same parents and grew up in the same home. Each however, has made a different choice at some point in their lives. Those choices sent them in opposite directions; Uncle John in the direction of a life of adventure, and Billy's father in the direction of an average family man. One is not better than the other—just different, and both had to give up something in order to live the life they chose. Were they both happy with their choices? You decide. Did one envy the other? You'll have to read the poem. As you read the poem, think about what kind of person you are and answer the same questions about yourself. Are you happy with your choices? Do you envy another person? Are you an "achiever" or a "dreamer"? It may start you thinking. I know I did.

Please, for your reading pleasure, enjoy—"The Visit."

---

*A sailor visits his brother's family. Both the sailor and his brother
learn something about themselves, and each other.*

THE VISIT

There was a knock at the door,
And from the outside came a yell.
Is there a room for a sailor here,
To rest his bones a spell?

To the front door little Billy ran,
As he screamed at the top of his voice.
It's Uncle John home from sea.
It was truly a time to rejoice.

Billy's father leaped from his chair,
As excited as Billy was he.
Billy's mother ran down from up-stairs,
To welcome Uncle John home from sea.

Uncle John was standing there,
Pipe in mouth and sea bag in hand.
Seaman's cap and pea-coat he wore,
He was a mountain of a man.

His face was weathered. His hands were chapped.
He had a touch of gray in his hair.
His voice was loud. He always laughed.
All knew Uncle John was there.

Yes, Uncle John was a special man.
He had a swagger to his walk.
Bigger than life with his stories of the sea.
For hours we listened to him talk.

Little Billy said, Tell me some stories.
As he climbed up in Uncle John's lap.
Uncle John smiled, and winked at Billy's father.
Billy's father smiled, and winked back.

I'll tell you some stories of the sea I love.
When you grow-up you may love the sea too.
They are strange stories and hard to believe,
But trust me—they are all true.

Uncle John then told of adventures at sea,
And creatures that he has seen.
The eyes of Billy grew wider and wider.
They sparkled with an innocent gleam.

Uncle John then told of giant squid and whales,
And porpoise that swam his bow wave.
Of exotic islands and gorgeous sunsets,
And anchoring in beautiful bays.

I wish you could see those island girls.
His throat, Billy's father then cleared.
Uncle John stopped, clearing his throat he said,
I'll tell you those stories, in a few years.

This went on for three full days.
It was like a party, and time flew by fast.
Uncle John then said it was time to leave.
I could get only, a three day pass.

Billy's Father told John if he would like,
To the ship he would walk with him.
John said thanks, but a shipmate would come,
And at a bar, their elbows they would bend.

Uncle John then laughed and hugged Billy's father.
And said a man can get mighty thirsty at sea.
We're sailing tomorrow I'll be at sea for a while.
I need to wet my whistle, before I leave.

Shortly after that a seaman knocked at the door.
He said I'm looking for big John is he here?
Good-byes were said, and Uncle John hugged Billy.
Then said to the seaman—"let's get a beer."

John and the seaman walked out the door,
And the house seemed empty and sad.
The eyes of Billy's father filled with tears,
For more time with John, he would like to have.

Billy's mother kissed his father on the cheek,
And said he's quite-a-brother you know.
Billy's father said he's a one of a kind.
I sure hate to see my brother go.

Billy's mother whispered to his father.
You would love to be like him wouldn't you?
Who wouldn't" Billy's father quickly replied.
If you were a man, you would too.

Uncle John and the seaman walked towards the street.
For the first time no laughter was heard.
With tears in his eyes John turned and waved good-bye.
No one—said a word.

We heard the seaman tell Uncle John.
Your brother seems like a lucky man to me.
Uncle John replied wiping tears from his eyes.
The luckiest man on earth—I wish, I was he.

                                  Cleon McClain

Glenda's All American Redheads photo—1974

CH. 13

Commentary on "Me, My Brother, and Friend"

I was looking at a couple of old Polaroid pictures of my brother, a friend of mine, and me. The picture was taken over thirty-five years ago. We were sailing the second sailboat I ever owned. It was a Columbia 22. The boat had a sun-faded red hull and a chalky sun-bleached white deck. Needless to say, it was not in pristine condition by any stretch of the imagination. But, I could not have been more proud of that boat if it were an America's Cup racing yacht. I noticed how so very young and happy we were in the picture. I also remembered how close the three of us were to each other.

My friends' name is Jerry MacLean. We have been friends since 6th grade. We drifted apart for a short time after high school, when he went to college in Nebraska, and I stayed in Oklahoma to go to college. He now lives in a suburb of Kansas City, and I in a small town in Oklahoma. Throughout all these years, we have stayed in close contact with each other. We talk on the phone weekly and visit several times throughout the year.

My brother and I live about forty-five miles away from each other. We visited often until about two years ago. Our relationship is now strained because of a family issue, and we seldom talk to each other, except to take care of family business. It's a sad arrangement, but not unlike many families these days.

Looking at the pictures the memories filled my head. I remember how in those days we were inseparable. We spent most of our waking hours together. Never did three young men have a closer relationship than we. Like the Mary Hopkin song said "Those were the days."

As I continued to look at the pictures, I remembered how carefree we were. Not only were we young, but our parents, friends, aunts, uncles, and cousins were young as well. It seemed the whole world would never grow old and time would never end. Everything, and every day, was a new adventure for us.

As I reminisced over those pictures, I felt the need to put all this in a poem and that is how "Me, My Brother, and Friend" was conceived.

"Me, My Brother, and Friend" is a poem about that special relationship we had in those days. The poem tells of the three of us in the prime of our lives going on a weekend sailing adventure. It was a typical sailing trip we often took down Lake Tenkiller, which is located in northeastern Oklahoma.

In those days we never thought of wearing life jackets, for we were young and thought we were invincible. Our favorite game was trailing a long line from the back of the boat, while taking turns jumping off the bow. We would then catch the line trailing from the boat as it sailed past us. We then would pull ourselves to the boat and climb the stern ladder to re-board, that is, unless someone as a joke pulled in the line to leave you stranded in the lake, treading water. We would then have to do our man overboard drill, and turn the boat around to pick up the stranded swimmer. Yes, we were young and like most young men we did some dumb things, and although it's a wonder we did not kill ourselves, it was all in fun and that was what we were all about. I could go on for hours telling of the things we did in those days, but the best way I know for this old man to reminisce about sailing, and friendships of his youth is through a poem.

Please, for your reading pleasure, enjoy—"Me, My Brother, and Friend."

An old man reminisces about the time his brother, friend, and he went on a weekend sailing trip.

ME, MY BROTHER, AND FRIEND

Although it happened years ago,
It seems like yesterday.
When we shoved off from the dock,
Eager to sail away.

We were all so very young,
Without a care in the world.
Our boat heeled and gathered speed,
As the main unfurled.

We sailed a Columbia 22.
Under a sun filled sky.
With clouds that looked like cotton-balls.
That slowly drifted by.

The jib was hoisted, our boat jumped.
As if awakening from sleep.
I felt the power of our boat.
Beneath my two bare feet.

The sun reflected off the water,
Sparkling brilliant blue.
I was captain of the boat.
My brother and friend was crew.

We were like the three Musketeers.
Inseparable you might say.
Before time passed and we grew-up,
And went our separate ways.

In those days the only thing,
We thought of was having fun.
As we sailed across the lake,
Under the summer sun.

Down the lake to the dam,
Where we would spend the night.
But lots of sailing we had to do,
While it was still daylight.

We laughed and played and joked around,
And sails occasionally trimmed.
We would all run to the bow,
And take turns diving in.

We had a line that we had tied,
Trailing from the boat.
We'd grab the line, climb back on-board,
As we laughed and joked.

We played this game and horsed around,
For the longest time.
Sailing down this care free lake,
With only fun in mind.

Oh, how I cherish these memories,
Of days long ago.
They are more precious to me now,
Than silver, platinum, or gold.

My brother I remember,
Was on the bow ready to dive.
Pointing to the water he yelled,
Look quickly to port-side.

In the water beneath the boat,
Was a school of fish.
He then dove into the lake,
They scattered with a swish.

He dragged himself back to the boat,
On the line that trailed.
As he climbed back in boat,
My friend then suddenly yelled.

Look the fish have all swam back,
To the boat he cheered.
The fish then swam around the boat,
Then suddenly, disappeared.

We reached the dam to spend the night,
Just as we had hoped.
We rocked asleep in our bunks,
Gently by the boat.

The night was calm. The sky was black,
Except for twinkling stars.
We dreamed the dreams sailors dream,
When they sail afar.

The next morning we awoke,
Ready for the day.
We knew the weekend would soon end,
But that would be okay.

For we were young with lots of time,
Everything was a game.
But now that I am old and gray,
Time is everything.

We had to sail back up the lake,
Against the summer wind.
And we continued to laugh and play,
Like this would never end.

When we could finally see the dock,
From where we sailed yesterday.
We decided to stow the motor
Sailing all the way.

As we sailed to the dock,
We dropped our jib as planned.
Sailing under main alone,
All hands on deck I command.

I luffed the main, and steered the boat
Slowly toward the dock.
The crew jumped off and grabbed the boat.
We came to a perfect stop.

Those days now, have come and gone.
I think of them now I'm old.
We were so young and full of life.
Where did all that time go?

Days turn to years, years to decades,
But I'll never forget that weekend.
When the three of us set sail that day,
Just me, my brother, and friend.

        Cleon McClain

Cleon's brother aboard his Columbia 22—1975

CH. 14

Commentary on "Eleven Tears of the Lord"

When I was in the sixth grade, I was given a school assignment to write a limerick. This was the first time I ever tried my hand at poetry. The name of my limerick was "The Little Ball."

The Little Ball

> Once there was a little ball.
> Who was more round than he was tall.
> He had not the nerve.
> To build up a curve.
> And so when thrown he would fall.
>
> Cleon McClain—1965

Five years later, I was seventeen years old and a junior in high school. I was given an assignment to write my next poem. This time it was not to write a limerick, but a "real poem." I wrote "Eleven Tears of the Lord." This is the only poem in the selection that is not about sailors or sailing adventures, but it is so special to me I just had to include it in my book. It is also not a coincidence that this is the last poem in my book. I thought it would be fitting to end my poetry with the first poem I ever wrote; to complete the circle so to speak, by ending where I first began.

I remember the day I wrote "Eleven Tears of the Lord." It was a rare thing for me to be absent from school, but I did miss school on that day because I was sick. I then wrote this poem while I was in bed recovering.

I was so very young, but even at that young age I had an interest in astronomy. To this day, I am very interested in astronomy, and now own several telescopes and a small observatory in my backyard. I've even had the privilege of teaching astronomy at the high school level.

Growing up my family and I believed in God, but we did not attend church. So at that time in my life, I was struggling with my own spirituality. I think this struggle continues throughout life, but this struggle can be particularly difficult for young people, who are trying to find some kind of spiritual identity. I know it was for me.

This was also in 1970. We had just come through the turbulent sixties with all the tragedies and accomplishments of that decade. The assassinations of the Kennedys and Martin Luther King, civil unrest, race riots, the Vietnam war, the draft, landing a man on the moon, and Woodstock. The list could go on and on. It was enough to make your head swim. To a seventeen year old like me, there was a lot to think about, but this was the world we lived in at that time. The poem "Eleven Tears of the Lord" was my attempt to express my faith, while incorporating my interest in astronomy, and dealing with many of the issues at that time. Today when I read the poem I see a lot of changes I would make, but that would spoil the poem. For this is not the poem that an old man like me would write, but rather the poem of a young seventeen year old living in the world in 1970. Yes, when I read the poem, I don't see myself as I am, but rather how I was. I was a young man trying to make sense of a rapidly changing world and trying to figure out how I was going to fit into it.

For years I thought this poem was lost forever. I remembered writing the poem, but like most of my school assignments, once I received the grade they usually ended up in the trash can. I always thought this was the fate of my poem. Then, when my grandfather passed away in 1995 at the age of 96, my mother found the poem in his house. Evidently, I gave my grandparents a copy of the poem, which they cared enough about to save. So, only through the thoughtfulness of my grandparents did this poem survive. My parents did not tell me about this and they had the poem framed and gave it to me the next Christmas as a present. The poem now hangs on the wall in the entrance of my home.

After writing "Eleven Tears of the Lord", over forty years passed before I again put pen to paper and tried my hand at poetry. I then wrote "Old Man in a Rocking Chair." I still do not understand why I felt the need to suddenly express myself through poetry so late in my life. I was never particularly interested in poetry, outside the reading of greeting cards. Throughout my adult life my interest has been in science and sailing. Consequently, most all the reading I have done has been in those areas. However, one day for a reason I can't explain, I sat down and started writing a poem about sailing. As I have mentioned that poem became "Old Man in a Rocking Chair." The writing of sailing poems then just started to become a part of me. One poem seemed to spawn an idea for the next. Eventually, these poems became the book you are now reading.

As I read "Eleven Tears of the Lord" I think about the young man that wrote the poem. I think about the time he lived and what was going on at that time. If you are old enough to remember those times, take a few minutes and reminisce. Maybe you even wrote a poem in your English class. Now might be a good time to get it out of that old shoebox in the closet and read it. I promise it will bring back memories that you probably haven't thought about in years.

If you are young, you can only listen to the older people tell the stories of those times, or read about them in history books. I urge you to do this. In particular listen to the stories of your parents and grandparents, for this is your heritage that needs to be passed on to your children.

I would also like to remind the young people to understand that all the old people of today were once young and vibrant like you. Also, understand that your youth is only temporary and will not last forever. Someday you too will be old. Time moves fast and the older you get the faster it seems to move. It has been said that youth is wasted on the young. This is true for all of us, no matter our age, for we are all younger today than we will be tomorrow. We should never take life for granted, and cherish every minute we have remaining, before God calls us home.

Please, for your reading pleasure, enjoy my first poem—"Eleven Tears of the Lord."

The Lord cries.

ELEVEN TEARS OF THE LORD

The Lord looked over empty space.
He thought I'll make the human race.
But where shall I put them? He sat down to sigh.
Then one little tear dropped from his right eye.

Earth was formed from that tiny tear.
The first of many to find their way here.
Then the Lord saw the very first sin.
He sat down and thought of His little men.

What should I do? He sat down to cry.
But only one tear dropped from His red eye.
Pluto was born from His second tear.
A planet so small and not very near.

The Lord saw wars, blood and death.
And when He sat down to catch His breath;
Only one tear, fell when He cried.
Neptune was born from this drop of pride.

Still people died, and still people bled.
Things got worse, the hills turned red.
The Lord cried again, another tear fell.
Uranus popped up from under the spell.

As He looked down into the sin,
He saw some good, deep within.
A tear of joy, the fifth that fell,
Jupiter was born, this was well.

The Lord wanted a Son of His very own.
Jesus was born in a stable alone.
Another tear fell and the Lord said,
There's Saturn's halo around My Son's head.

For His Father, Jesus died on a cross.
The Lord saw Him pay a terrible cost.
Another tear fell, the seventh did fall.
A red planet was formed, Mars it's called.

As the Lord looked, He saw nothing but bad.
The more He thought, the more He grew sad.
Another tear fell, and Mercury was born.
The closest to Sun, it'll always be warm.

Things got worse, as time went by.
Then from the Lord's blood-shot eye;
One more tear, the ninth that fell.
It burned a pit, that we call Hell.

But He still saw good in a few of His men.
They'll be with Him, for always my friends.
Venus was born from His tenth tear.
This planet will always be close and dear.

For those very few, that are good and kind,
He will always keep a special place in His mind.
He cried a tear, it was number eleven.
He'll make a place for them, in His Heaven.

> Cleon McClain, 1970

Cleon's high school senior picture—1971

APPENDICES

Introduction

Several of the poems in this book were written with my current sailboat the *Glenda Kay* in mind. In the poem "The Conversation" I directly make reference to the *Glenda Kay*. Also, much of what is written in the poem "Autumn Evening" occurred while in the tiny cockpit of the *Glenda Kay*.

Poetry is more than just the reading of words. Poetry is also a visual experience. The mental image that is conjured up in one's mind is very important in making a poem come "alive" and often gives the poem meaning. With this in mind, I thought you might enjoy reading about how I came to own my current sailboat the *Glenda Kay*, as well as a couple of my sailing adventures with her. The following are three articles in which all, or part, have been previously published in *Small Craft Advisor* magazine. It is my hope that these stories will make the reading of my poems a more pleasurable experience for you, and maybe even entice you to read some of the poems a second time.

Please, for your reading pleasure, enjoy the true stories of the *Glenda Kay*.

Cleon McClain

The *Glenda Kay*—2004

The Glenda Kay

In 1975, I saw a Guppy 13 for the first time at the Tulsa Boat Sport and Travel Show. I remember two men looking at it and laughing. One asked the other, "Is it a boat or a bath tub?" I wondered how they could be so disrespectful as to talk about this beautiful little boat like that. For me it was love at first sight. I saw the boat as a beautiful little yacht with a sweet personality that would make even the most cynical smile. Of all the boats in the boat show, this little boat captured my imagination, but was beyond my financial reach.

At that time I owned a Columbia 22 and was just graduating from college. I was up to my eyeballs in debt and could not afford to buy another boat. But, I knew this was the boat for me . . . someday. I never forgot that pretty little sailboat resting in a tiny cradle at the boat show that day.

After graduation, I became a teacher and for several years continued to sail. Then due to circumstances, I sold my sailboats and stopped sailing. I married my wife Glenda and before I knew it, years—then decades passed.

I was now one year away from retirement. I had often talked to Glenda about the little sailboat I saw so many years ago. I could not remember the exact length, but I never forgot the name "Guppy."

One day my wife called to me. She had found a Guppy 13 website on the computer. She asked, "Is this the boat you're always talking about?" There it was—the first Guppy 13 I had seen in decades! My mouth dropped. I recognized it immediately. I could not believe my eyes.

Through the years, I had talked to sailboat dealers and none could remember a boat called a Guppy. As I read the computer monitor, I understood why. The Guppy 13 was only in production for two years,

1974 and 1975. Now I could afford a Guppy, but the problem would be finding one.

I emailed all the Guppy owners on the website and asked if they knew where I could find a Guppy. I was about to give up hope when I received a response from Warren and Elizabeth. Warren would not be able to sail anymore, due to a back injury. They said they would be interested in selling their Guppy for $1,800. I could tell Warren hated to let his little boat go, but this was my chance. I was so excited I did not even make a counter offer.

The name of the boat was *Tweety*. She was in South Carolina and we live in Muskogee, Oklahoma. Distance was not going to keep me from the sailboat I waited for so many years to own. Within a week my wife and I were on our way.

We arrived back home on July 4, 2003, stopping as we passed through our neighborhood to show off the latest member of our family. *Tweety* was a gem. She was in great condition for a lady nearly 30 years of age. I set to work giving *Tweety* a facelift. I pampered *Tweety* by giving her everything from a new painted cabin to replacing her old tired rigging and giving her a new set of yellow sails. Like a butterfly, *Tweety* was ready to emerge from her cocoon . . . almost.

It was time to make one last change in my boat. In honor of my wife, who had been so supportive of the renovation of *Tweety*, it was time to pay tribute. I decided to put all superstitions about changing a boat's name aside. *Tweety's* name now was officially changed to the "*Glenda Kay*," after my wife. The transformation was complete.

I know the *Glenda Kay* does not sparkle like the new boat I saw in 1975 at the boat show, but the years have given her character and personality. She still has the charm to put smiles on faces as we tow her down the road, or as she gracefully dances across a lake. She gives me pride each time her keel slips into the water. I know she will always act like the distinguished lady she has become, and I hope to always be a worthy skipper. The *Glenda Kay* gives my wife and me more pleasure than we deserve. The *Glenda Kay* proved to me that old dreams can come true after all, if you just keep dreaming.

The *Glenda Kay*—2008

Sailing Greenleaf Lake

I turned off of state highway 10 and began a careful lookout for wildlife. I had traveled this road many times and I knew I was likely to see deer, wild turkey, armadillo, or other wild animals.

The anticipation and wondering what may be seen around the next bend always makes this drive a delight. I had entered Greenleaf State Park, located in northeastern Oklahoma, my favorite lake to sail.

Soon I began the descent down a winding road. A moment later I could see the blue water sparkling through the trees. The view was spectacular and never fails to take my breath away, but for some reason the colors of the panorama appeared more vivid than usual. I could smell the fragrance of the lake as the breeze filtered through the trees. Streaks of golden sunlight penetrated the shadows of the forest and the grandeur of nature was amplified as to overwhelm my senses. I then knew this was the right place for me, and this sailing trip was going to be memorable.

Every sailor has a special lake, island, or lagoon that inspires their dreams. Greenleaf Lake is mine. It is a small lake, and not a lake from which to set sail with the hope of reaching a particular destination. Instead, Greenleaf is the destination. Secluded, peaceful, and pristine, that's Greenleaf Lake.

 Continuing down the winding road, I soon reached Greenleaf's only marina. As usual, it looked like I was going to have the lake all to myself, for I could not see another boat on the lake. These are the conditions I've come to expect, for I have been spoiled by the serenity of this lake.

My boat, the *Glenda Kay* was rigged and water ready with little fuss. A few more minutes to stow my provisions and we were ready to back down the short boat-ramp. To my surprise, I found the boat-ramp at that moment was occupied by about fifteen Canadian geese. Not being in a hurry, I decided to yield to my feathered friends and retreat to the marina restaurant to grab a bite to eat. The burger, chips, and coke hit the spot but the geese were still camped-out on the boat ramp. They swam off loudly scolding me as I backed my boat into the lake. The *Glenda Kay* appeared to leap off her trailer into the familiar water. It was as if she was telling me that she was as excited as I to finally get started on our overnight trip. We set sail with no agenda and in no hurry. Our mission was simple, to relax, enjoy the moment, and sail.

Like many lakes in Northeastern Oklahoma, Greenleaf is narrow and winds its way through a valley that is skirted by steep hills with lush vegetation. However, because Greenleaf is so small this can make for very busy sailing. This is especially true when tacking to windward. Often the wind seems to change speed and direction with each bend in the lake, and is one of the challenges that I have grown to enjoy.

Deciding to sail the length of the lake, I headed northeast directly into a moderate wind. I knew this would take some time because of the very short tacks I would have to make, but I was not in a hurry. Sailing under main and working jib we began the task. I could see signs of high winds being funneled down the middle of the lake about one-hundred yards wide with calmer water on each side closer to the banks. The waves do not get very high on Greenleaf because the lake is small, but the wind that is funneled through the valley can be tricky. Sure-enough, as we passed through the middle of the lake the wind was very intense. Then, suddenly the wind moderated as we closed in on the other bank. A moment later we made a port tack to repeat the process. I had to tack about every ten minutes, and each time fight that one section of very high wind. Four or five tacks later, I decided to drop the jib and have a more leisurely sail. After all, the whole idea of the trip was to relax. Now I was sailing much slower and could not point to windward as well, but I was enjoying every minute.

The scenery slowly changed as I rounded each bend. The time seemed to fly by, and I was absorbing all the sights, sounds, and smells of nature. I watched the birds soaring overhead and inhaled the pungent aquatic aroma of the lake. The water gurgled past my rudder as we sailed under a brilliant blue sky. I thought about how rich I am, maybe not financially, but in a kind of wealth that cannot be bought. It was a magical moment.

Afternoon was turning to evening, and the funnel of wind blowing down the middle of the lake was dying down. I decided it was time to raise the jib. I could tell the *Glenda Kay* was happy to be fully dressed again. She immediately responded with a lurch forward, and we started making good time once more. We were reaching the upper end of the lake now, and I was starting to think of where to spend the night.

Deciding to spend the night in a cove across from the marina, we turned around to begin the run down the lake. Now the wind was working to our advantage, and was welcomed as it carried us wing-n-wing down the lake. The yellow sails were stretched tight on each side of the mast, and the evening sun made them appear to glow. It was a beautiful sight and a most pleasant run. The heat of the day was starting to cool and I was looking forward to the sanctuary of the little cove where we would spend the night.

I dropped anchor at about eight o'clock in the evening. The sun was slowly sinking in the west and the sky became ablaze with color. As I ate dinner I noticed a beaver swimming by. I unknowingly had anchored near a beaver lodge. Watching these magnificent animals was an unexpected treat, as we were enveloped by the metamorphosis from day to night. The wind died to a calm making the water like a mirror that reflected the light of the stars, as they began to appear one by one. The night noises seemed to be amplified as they echoed through the calm of the night. I crawled into the tiny cabin feeling a tremendous pride for my little boat. I knew the *Glenda Kay* would be working while I slept, keeping me dry and safe from the elements throughout the night. This was the perfect end to a perfect day.

At about midnight I was awakened by light coming through the clear plexiglass companion-way door. Opening the hatch, I poked my head out of the tiny cabin. The moon was almost full and had finally risen above the surrounding mountains. It was so bright that shadows were produced. Seldom in my life have I seen the moon that radiant, as the light was reflected over the calm lake. The total stillness and absolute silence was eerie, and the moment seemed almost sacred. It was one of those rare times that can never be anticipated, and never forgotten.

It was an unusually cool June night and the morning air was crisp. I was going to meet my wife, Glenda, at the marina around 8:30 this morning to take her sailing. It was calm and the lake was smooth as glass, so I started the motor and was tied up at the dock by 8:00 a.m. Glenda had not arrived yet, but it felt good to walk around and stretch my legs for a few minutes. It was not long before Glenda's smiling face appeared. We ate a small breakfast at the marina restaurant and waited for the wind. Soon the wind came and we set sail. The wind was perfect. The sun was shining, and the sky was the color of blue that is usually seen only in pictures. Glenda and I continued to sail and visit for hours. Time seemed to stand still. But, all too soon our day of sailing in paradise was coming to an end. It was now time to sail back to the marina.

Knowing the trip was coming to an end, Glenda and I decided to take one last walk around the park. We walked past the heated fishing dock to the Greenleaf Nature Center. The nature center features wildlife found in northeastern Oklahoma. The exhibit we liked best was a small baby deer. It was covered with spots and leaped from one side of his pen to the other to be petted by laughing children and admired by the adults. The center also had two baby raccoons with black masks like bank robbers. They put on a show chasing each other, as if they were playing a game of tag. The unmistakable backdrop of our walk was always the beauty of the lake. I don't think I could ever tire of looking at it. We ended our walk back at the marina where it all began.

Before I knew it our time on Greenleaf Lake had come to an end. I could sense sadness from my little boat, as she slipped from the gentle lake onto her hard trailer. I too was caught by the spell of this enchanted lake, and the thought of leaving gave me a feeling of emptiness. The siren-song of Greenleaf is strong, and I couldn't help but sneak one last peek at the serene little lake before starting the trip back home.

God willing, I will drop anchor many more times in the sparkling water of Greenleaf, but now, I look out my bedroom window and see the *Glenda Kay* resting sadly under the carport on her trailer. I close my eyes and dream about the little boat I've come to love. She's in crystal clear water with a gentle breeze filling her yellow sails. Green hills surround her as she dances under a deep blue sky. *Glenda Kay* is once again happy, sailing across a tiny lake in northeastern Oklahoma, named Greenleaf.

Greenleaf Lake—2009

Lake Tenkiller Adventure

Our small caravan consisted of my truck pulling our thirteen-foot sailboat, the *Glenda Kay,* and my wife Glenda following in her car. Our new boat was nearly thirty years old, and it had been almost that many years since I last sailed. I was nervous, but the *Glenda* Kay had an air of confidence about her as we rolled down the highway. We were in route to Cherokee Landing on Lake Tenkiller in Northeastern Oklahoma.

The lake was beautiful, but the water level was very low due to the severe drought. It was just matter of minutes before we had our little sailboat rigged with all the supplies stowed and backing down a long, long boat-ramp. A moment later, the *Glenda Kay* was bobbing in the lake just as happy as a duck on a pond. My wife was on shore taking pictures. I was doing what no sailor that had taken a thirty year sabbatical from sailing should ever do—showing off. The lake was fairly calm with a moderate wind. I was waving for the camera. Suddenly, a gust of wind caught me by surprise. My little boat heeled over rapidly. I was so startled I didn't know what to do. I did not want to look scared in front of my wife who was taking pictures, or endure the humiliation of being capsized within minutes of the trip. Trying to look as calm as possible, I immediately dropped the jib, and nonchalantly waved for the camera, and yelled good-bye to my wife. The next thing I knew, I saw my wife waving to me from her car as she drove off, while I was in a state of confusion sailing down the lake under main alone, with the jib flapping on the tiny deck.

The wind was starting to kick-up from the northeast in the direction I was running down the lake. I could tell by the size of the waves, which were now starting to whitecap that I needed to take a reef in the mainsail. I also wanted to stow the jib that I hastily dropped on my departure. This is not an easy task on a twelve foot boat in choppy wave conditions such as these. I needed to find some shelter out of the main body of the lake. The closest was Northeastern Cove. The wind continued to increase in strength, and I was starting to become very concerned. The wind was now putting a significant strain on the rigging, and the *Glenda Kay* was not in a happy mood. When I finally reached the sanctuary of the cove, I dropped the main and set there for a long moment to collect my thoughts. In my younger days when I was doing a lot of sailing, I would have been ready to get back out in the lake to see what the *Glenda Kay* had in her keel. However now, I am not nearly as quick to take chances as I was in my youth. I also did not have the confidence in my sailing ability that I once had. From the calm of the cove, I could see the whitecaps out in the main body of the lake. Because of pride, I knew going back was not an option—I made the decision. I stowed the jib, put a reef in the main sail, took a deep breath, and headed back into the wind and waves on the lake. I was so happy to see how well the *Glenda Kay* was sailing. I realized I had broken one of the first rules of sailing- never wait too long before reducing sail.

The lake at this point turned 90 degrees to the west. A mountain blocked most of the wind and made for a pleasant beam reach. It was nice to be able to sit back, relax, and enjoy the beautiful scenery. I got a bottle of water out of the cooler, and with reduced sail, was just ghosting over the calm water in a mild breeze. I was totally enjoying the slow movement of the *Glenda Kay* as we sliced through the mirror reflections in the water. My mind, while taking in this serene beauty, could not help but reflect back on the breath-taking run that I had just made. This is what I love about sailing, never knowing what marvelous adventures might be ahead and allowing the sailor to ride the wind and experience the wonders of nature. Sometimes I get the wits scared out of me, but most of the time, sailing is so sublime as to be almost a religious experience.

My first destination was to be Pettit Bay Marina. I could see the lake was going to tee-off with Pettit Bay up a very large cove to the north and the main body of the lake bending to the south. As I approached the bend and sailed out from behind the mountain that had been sheltering me, the wind began to pick up. I saw some ripples in the lake. Then WHAM! It hit me again, a very hard wind. I was glad I did not shake the reef out of my sail. Although the sudden wind caught me by surprise, I was in pretty good shape. I pointed the *Glenda Kay* into the wind getting ready to beat my way up to the marina, when I saw a stump just under the water. I also noticed several old trees standing in the shallow water and decided it would be wiser to drop the main sail and motor to the marina.

Arriving at Pettit Bay Marina, I found it was closed. The cockpit of the *Glenda Kay* is very small, about the size of a bathtub. This was a good opportunity to take a short walk and stretch my legs, before sailing on to my next destination, Six-Shooter Marina. I motored out of Pettit Bay, hoisted the reefed main sail, and continued down the lake.

The run down to Six-Shooter took just under two hours. I was glad I decided to keep the reef in the main and not hoist the jib, because the sailing conditions remained the same. I would run before very high wind, with white-capped waves. It was very exciting and most exhilarating. I had to pay very close attention to prevent an accidental gybe and broach. This took my full concentration. Then the lake would bend, putting me on a beam reach in the lee of the mountains and I would enjoy some very relaxing sailing. This continued until I reached Six-Shooter Marina. The *Glenda Kay* seemed to be happy and not complaining. I was also regaining some of my old sailing confidence.

Arriving at Six-Shooter, I had a soda and took another walk. The marina attendant told me that Tinker Cove would be a good place to anchor for the night. It was across the lake and would have a "no wake" buoy at the mouth of it. "You can't miss it" said the attendant. So, a plan was made—I would spend the night at Tinker Cove.

After sailing for about an hour, I decided the attendant over estimated my navigation abilities. Tinker Cove was nowhere to be seen! Then suddenly the "no wake" buoy appeared. It was a very large cove, with a narrow mouth, and entirely surrounded by mountains. It was beautiful. The perfect spot to anchor the *Glenda Kay* for the night! I took some pictures, went for a swim, ate dinner, and prepared for the night.

I crawled into the tiny cabin leaving the hatch open, lying on my back watching the mast as it moved in small circles under the cloud covered sky. Soon I was asleep. At about 3:00 a.m. I was startled when I felt the boat suddenly shake, accompanied with a loud sound, like someone threw a rock and hit one of the stays. Immediately I poked my head out of the cabin. Just inches from my nose, I saw a bat staggering around on the top of the cabin next to the mast. As I pondered what to do, the bat regained its senses and flew away. It was then that I witnessed one of the most incredible sights I have ever seen. What must have been thousands of fireflies illuminated my surroundings. The tiny phosphorescent light emitted from each individual firefly, twinkling off and then on, made for a visual extravaganza. The effect was hypnotic. The longer I watched the more I wanted to see. I had somehow been invited to witness a magical land that is usually found only in the innocent imagination of children. It was like being in one of those 3-D movies, only this time I was not just watching, but actually a part of it. Then I figured out what must have happened. The bat must have been feeding on these fireflies when it hit one of my stays and fell on the cabin top. How grateful I am to this little bat for giving me this once in a lifetime opportunity. I crawled back into the tiny cabin and fell asleep watching thousands of twinkling fireflies under a cloud covered sky. It was a magical night that I will never forget.

I awoke to a beautiful sunny day. The wind was very light from the north, with a calm lake. I hoisted the main and jib and with the *Glenda Kay* fully dressed, began the long beat back to Cherokee Landing.

I decided I would sail for Barnacle Bill's Marina, get some ice, and give my wife a call. It was very slow sailing. The scenery was spectacular with high wooded bluffs reflecting off the crystal clear water and mares' tails drifting across an otherwise blue sky. The *Glenda Kay* sailed from one side of the lake to the other, each time tacking a little closer to our final destination. How different today was from the white-knuckle sailing we were doing just yesterday. Suddenly a small airplane circled low overhead. I began to wave at the pilot who waved back by tipping his wings, as is the custom of aviators as he flew off.

What an extraordinary trip this has been! The wind was starting to pick-up and Barnacle Bill's Marina was in sight. Thirty minutes later, sails were dropped and we motored into the marina.

Upon arriving at the marina I noticed it looked deserted. Sure enough, just as I experienced at Pettit Bay Marina the day before, it was closed. Although most of the ice in my cooler had melted, the water was still very cold, so ice was of little importance. Also, if things went the way I planned, I would be home by the end of the day so the phone call to Glenda was really not necessary. The thing for me to do was to get on with the business of sailing back to Cherokee Landing.

We sailed away from Barnacle Bill's into very calm waters. The sailing was extremely slow. The wind had been increasing throughout the morning and the conditions I was now enjoying was deceptive, due to being on the lee side of a very long mountain. I could see at the end of the mountain around the next bend that the lake was showing signs of very rough water. I decided I was going to keep both sails up, sheet them in tight, and point as close as possible into the wind. For once, things went just as planned. As I rounded the bend, the wind hit us with a great force. This time I was ready. I pointed the *Glenda Kay* into the wind and started to beat our way up the lake. The lake had whitecaps and I was getting soaked by the spray from the bow. It was very tense and the *Glenda Kay* was working hard, but did not seem to be complaining. I was starting to wonder if I was making a mistake by carrying too much sail for these conditions. I could see the gusts of wind as they came across the lake. Each time one of the gusts hit us, I was able to point a little higher. Then just as the sails would start to luff, I would fall off a little and wait for the next gust. Then, repeat the process.

As I came up on the next bend in the lake, I expected to fall on the lee side of a mountain and have some easy sailing. Instead, the wind continued to blow very hard. I was now on a broad reach, and once again, carrying more sail than I would have liked. I seemed to be doing alright by slacking the main and allowing it to spill some of the wind. I was starting to get my old sailing confidence back and that's when it happened, the *Glenda Kay* suddenly was hit by a huge gust of wind that almost knocked us completely down. At this point everything seemed to start happening in slow motion, like you see at the movies as the plane crashes or the hero get shot. Only this time I was in the movie and it was real. I just knew I was going to sink my little *Glenda Kay*. I immediately doused the jib. The *Glenda Kay* was pointed into the wind with the main sail luffing and the doused jib flapping around on the deck, all making a tremendous noise. I was now at the next bend in the lake and needed to start tacking into the wind. I tried to beat to windward and the *Glenda Kay* was not responding. I could not get her to make any headway. With each tack I made to windward, I noticed we lost ground. If this continued we would soon be washed up on a lee shore. It was as if the *Glenda Kay* was telling me that she had had enough and was too tired to continue. We had just past Northeastern Cove, where the day before I had to stop and reduce sail. I decided enough was enough. I dropped the main sail and motored to College Cove.

College Cove is a long, narrow, and usually very beautiful cove. Now however, with the lake level low the cove has taken on a very different appearance. It was about 20 feet wide and 150 to 200 yards long. I motored to the back of the cove and anchored by tying lines from the bow and stern to opposite banks. This was now a very depressing cove. The water was stagnant with flies and the stench of dead fish filling the air. There was a scum over the top of the water and driftwood all around. The cove was calm and did give excellent shelter from the wind. For this, I was thankful. I checked out the *Glenda Kay* and she looked to be in better condition than me. I was emotionally drained, and although now stranded in this cesspool of a cove, did not have the courage to go back out into the main body of the lake.

I walked down the bank of the cove several times to check the condition of the lake with the same results, high winds and whitecaps. I resigned myself to the fact I was going to have to spend the night in the gloomy cove.

As I ate dinner I thought of what I could have done differently. The first thought was the obvious. I should have reefed the main early on. Secondly, I should not have dropped my jib so soon because I needed it to beat to windward. I would not have made these mistakes 30 years ago. Obviously, my sailing skills were not what they once were! In sailing conditions like these, decisions have to be made fast and correctly. I just hoped that I would not sink my *Glenda Kay* in the process of re-acquiring these skills. I was safe for now and so was the *Glenda Kay* and that was what mattered. I sat in the tiny cockpit and felt a since of pride for my little *Glenda Kay*. She must have had skippers (if that is what I could call myself) more skilled than I, but she is forgiving, and seems to be taking better care of me that I am of her!

That night I was lying in the cabin looking at the stars. They were breath taking. The Milky Way looked like some celestial river stretching across a diamond studded sky. The sight was beyond description. I then started thinking about my wife and sister-in-law warning me to be careful of snakes. I remember laughing and telling them I was not worried about being snake bitten in a sailboat. It's funny how your mind works. The night before in Tinker Cove, the thought of snakes never came into my mind. Now, lying in a cove that had the stench of rotting fish, snakes suddenly became all I thought about. I noticed even with the motor tilted up, part of its' shaft was still in the water. A snake could easily crawl up the shaft and get into the boat. I inserted the companionway door, hoping this would be enough deterrent to keep an uninvited reptile from slithering into my bed during the night. Each time I woke up, I would poke my head out the hatch and shine my flashlight up and down the shore. To my discomfort, twice I saw a snake lying on the bank next to the water. That was it! I decided I was going to leave in the morning at first light.

After a sleepless night I was ready to sail by 5:30 a.m. The only problem was no wind. The lake was as smooth as glass. It was cool with a fog rising from the lake. The sun was just starting to come up and it looked like a gorgeous day was developing. I made the decision not to wait any longer. It was time to get out of this miserable cove. I was going to motor back to Cherokee Landing. As I was starting to get the *Glenda Kay* underway, the snake that caused me to lose sleep swam by. I was happy to know that we would be miles apart tonight when my head hit the pillow. I ended my trip by motoring up the lake, watching as the sun painted the morning sky a breath taking red and orange. Thinking to myself, God has blessed me more than any man deserves.

The *Glenda Kay* at College Cove—2005

ABOUT THE AUTHOR

Cleon was born on January 12, 1953 in Tulsa, Oklahoma. He grew up in a middle class working family. His family consisted of an older brother, his mother who was a nurse, and a father who worked in the aviation industry. Cleon graduated high school in 1971 from East Central High School in Tulsa, and obtained a Bachelor of Science degree in biology and education in 1975 from Northeastern State University in Tahlequah, Oklahoma. He taught science for two years in the Tulsa Public School System and 28 years in the Fort Gibson Public School System. Cleon married his wife Glenda on November 22, 1986. They currently live in Muskogee, Oklahoma. Cleon retired from full-time teaching in 2004 and currently enjoys substitute teaching, sailing, astronomy, writing poetry, and spending time vacationing with Glenda and friends.

The author Cleon McClain and his wife Glenda—2012

Printed in Great Britain
by Amazon